SUPPLY CHAIN
Simplified

Dr. James Kirby Easterling

Kendall Hunt
publishing company

Cover Image: © Shutterstock.com

Kendall Hunt
publishing company

www.kendallhunt.com
Send all inquiries to:
4050 Westmark Drive
Dubuque, IA 52004-1840

Copyright © 2022 by Kendall Hunt Publishing Company

ISBN 979-8-7657-4219-8

Published in the United States of America

Dedication

To my wonderful wife and best friend, Teresa A. Easterling, who has stood faithfully with me *"through the years."* To my three daughters—Kourtney, Kassidy, and Kennedy—who have always been my source of motivation in tackling challenges, for *"as everybody knows...almost doesn't count."* In memory of my wonderful parents, James Franklin Easterling and Myrtle Marie Bentley Easterling, who instilled in me *"you've got to stand for something, or you'll fall for anything."* And in honor of a special uncle, Dr. Henry W. Easterling, Jr., who was a source of inspiration in tackling aspirational objectives and was always *"on the fightin' side for me"*. And in dedication to Dr. Bertee Adkins—an eastern Kentucky *"country boy"* like me—who, above all other professors, made a lasting difference in my life and the lives of countless other students teaching at Eastern Kentucky University. And finally, to my college students—past, present, and future—who have given me a new way to share my love of supply chain management in and outside the classrooms. *Glory to God from whom all blessings flow.* 1 CHRONICLES 16:34

Foreword

Sincere thanks for purchasing and reading my book. This book is neither a college textbook nor a dictionary; rather, it is intended for everyone from ages 15 to 95 with a desire to learn more about the <u>foundational</u> concepts of the exciting field of supply chain management. This book introduces key concepts with simple examples and lots of illustrations, tables, and pictures for heightened effect. You're going to learn hundreds of supply chain concepts in easy-to-understand language. You might even consider supply chain as a profession, as it's one of the hottest career tracks. Regardless of your reason for purchasing this book…happy reading!

Contents

About the author

Dr. James Kirby Easterling worked in progressive supply chain leadership and executive roles with multinational companies for over 20 years, including long-term international assignments in both Japan and Singapore with Corning Incorporated, before transitioning into academia in 2014, where he led the establishment of the Global Supply Chain Management program at Eastern Kentucky University. Easterling holds Bachelor of Business Administration degrees in both Economics and Accounting as well as an MBA from Eastern Kentucky University, a Master of Supply Chain Management degree from Pennsylvania State University, and a Doctor of Business Administration degree in Information Systems & Operations Management from the University of Florida. Easterling is currently Assistant Professor/Director of the Global Supply Chain Management program at Eastern Kentucky University.

© James Kirby Easterling

Contact information:

Dr. James Kirby Easterling
KirbyEasterling@gmail.com
859-779-5858

About the editor

Teresa L. Smith worked in supply chain roles for over 16 years in a variety of different industries, including owning her own transportation company for more than 10 years. Ms. Smith holds a Bachelor of Business Administration degree in Global Supply Chain Management from Eastern Kentucky University and a Master of Science degree in Supply Chain Management from Michigan State University, and she is now pursuing a Doctor of Business Administration degree at Marshall University. Ms. Smith is currently a Visiting Professor at Eastern Kentucky University, where she teaches undergraduate and graduate-level supply chain courses.

© Teresa L. Smith

Introduction to Supply Chain Management

Welcome to the exciting world of supply chain management (SCM), which is one of the hottest topics in the news. No doubt you've seen recent stories regarding how supply chain impacts our daily lives. Supply chain plays an essential role in supply and demand at all levels…local, state, national, and international. We can think about supply chain in the context of what is referred to as the ***perfect order***—getting the right product (or service), in the right quantity, in the right condition, at the right place, at the right time, to the right customer, at the right price.

© Corona Borealis Studio/shutterstock.com

When the *Ever Given* ocean container ship became stuck in the Suez Canal in 2021, it not only delayed the goods on that ship from being delivered, but hundreds of other container ships as well which had to take alternative, longer, and costlier routes.[1] Consumers saw price increases almost immediately, as basic economics illustrates that when there's a reduction in supply—without any corresponding reduction in demand—price increases will occur as customers compete for fewer resources. Sustained

---

[1] Anderson. J. (2021, May 17). 'Why Ships Crash' Review: Stuck in the Suez Canal. *The Wall Street Journal*. https://www.wsj.com/articles/why-ships-crash-review-stuck-in-the-suez-canal-why-ships-crash-nova-pbs-ever-given-suez-canal-2021-red-sea-modern-express-cosco-busan-el-faro-11652811845

price increases over a longer time frame are referred to as *inflation*. Without an increase in wages, sustained price increases lead to lower purchasing power for individuals. In a global economy, everything is interconnected. Supply chain is a lot like electricity—you don't fully appreciate it until it's not working correctly (or is working sub-optimally).

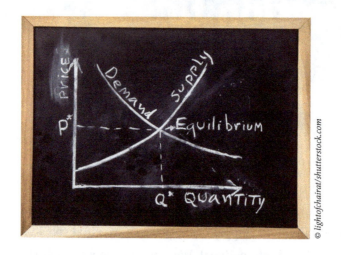

**"Supply Chain Management is the sequencing
of activities and organizations—
both internally and externally—
from order acceptance to order fulfillment"**

The terms *supply* and *demand* are constantly used in supply chain management. Supply is a combination of two elements: *inventory*, which is product that physically exists right now and is readily available to sell; and *capacity*, which is the ability to produce more output (or provide more service) in a period (for example, next month or next quarter). The combination of inventory and capacity is what supply chain professionals refer to as *Ability to Supply (ATS)*. We can apply the same logic to demand. Demand is also a combination of two elements: *customer orders*, which are formal (firm) commitments from customers (generally short-term oriented); and *forecasts*, which are estimates on what customers may want in the future (generally longer-term oriented).

Just as healthcare isn't comprised of any one task or job, supply chain management isn't any one singular thing either. Supply chain professionals work across a wide range of areas performing a wide range of roles. Thankfully, there's an overall framework for understanding the interrelated elements (or "pillars") called the *Supply Chain Operations Reference (SCOR) Model*.[2] The SCOR Model covers many facets of the exciting world of supply chain management, each of which we'll cover in depth in upcoming chapters.

---

[2] Association for Supply Chain Management. (n.d.). *SCOR model: introduction to processes*. https://scor.ascm.org/processes/introduction

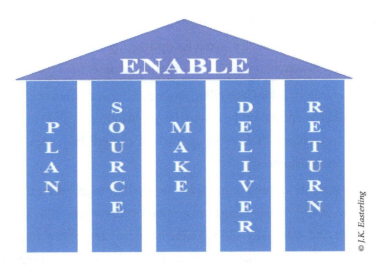

Let's apply the SCOR Model to one of America's great companies. Caterpillar Inc. was founded in 1925 and is the world's leading manufacturer of construction and mining equipment, diesel and natural gas engines, industrial gas turbines, and diesel-electric locomotives.[3] Caterpillar equipment comes in all shapes and sizes. Let's use Caterpillar as an example of SCOR considerations.

- **Plan:** How many different products will Caterpillar make? Will all products be offered in all markets? Are there targeted growth countries? What's the expected volume—now and in the future—for each product? Will new products (or enhancements) be developed, and if so, when?

- **Source:** Which components, subassemblies, and services will Caterpillar make internally (insource) versus purchase externally (outsource)? How will suppliers be selected? What criteria will be used for assessing suppliers? How will Caterpillar ensure suppliers act in ways consistent with the company's values?

---

[3] Caterpillar Inc. (n.d.). *About Caterpillar*. https://www.caterpillar.com/en/company.html

- **Make:** Will multiple Caterpillar products be made at each factory? What manufacturing processes will be used? What's the optimal facility layout for optimizing output? What's the degree of labor intensity versus equipment automation? How will quality be assured? What about worker safety?

- **Deliver:** How will raw materials for Caterpillar products be transported (rail, truck, ocean container ship)? Should transportation be insourced or outsourced? What are the weight limitations on roads and bridges where products are transported? How are Caterpillar products delivered to international customers?

A key point is that organizations need to integrate these pillars together for maximum effectiveness, much like gears in a fine watch. Supply chain integration occurs when all SCOR pillars are working together—both internally and externally—to maximize efficiencies, optimize customer service, and minimize total cost. We have an entire chapter dedicated to the importance of supply chain integration, as any given plan is only as good as those that follow it!

One of the key concepts in supply chain management is understanding that there are typically many companies and organizations involved in bringing a product (or service) to the marketplace, which is referred to as *end-to-end supply chain management*. Let's use aircraft engines as an example.

© Sopotnicki/shutterstock.com

An aircraft engine manufacturer (such as GE Aviation) sells engines to airplane manufacturers (such as Boeing), which is a business-to-business (B2B) transaction. Airplane manufacturers sell airplanes to airline companies (such as Delta), which is also a B2B transaction. Finally, Delta sells airplane tickets to <u>individual</u> customers, which is a business-to-consumer (B2C) transaction. However, airplane engines don't just magically appear. In fact, aircraft engines are comprised of more than 25,000 individual parts, and each one of those parts has a supplier(s) and a unique supply chain.

The illustration below highlights the major elements of an end-to-end supply chain for airplane engines. In this example, we focus on <u>one</u> of the key components of an aircraft engine—the fan blades. Fan blades are made from titanium, a mined natural resource. Keep in mind there are many other companies that participate in the end-to-end supply chain for aircraft engines in addition to those referenced below. Rolls-Royce and Pratt & Whitney, for example, also manufacturer aircraft engines. There are many other companies beyond Allegheny Technologies that mine titanium. The below illustration is simply meant to represent the various segments and participants in an end-to-end supply chain.

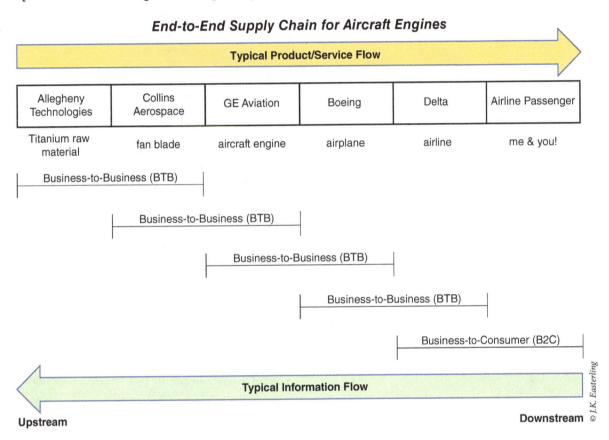

Illustrating an end-to-end supply chain in this manner highlights the major segments (i.e., organizations), as well as the B2B and B2C relationships. Other than individual airline passengers purchasing tickets, every other transaction is B2B. There's another more interesting aspect of the airplane engine illustration, which we discuss throughout this book: the concepts of **upstream** and **downstream**. Downstream always refers to the final customer (or consumer), while upstream refers to raw material suppliers (in this case titanium). So where does the supply chain "start"…with the titanium supplier or with the individual customer? The answer is that all supply chains start with the end customer, for without demand for air travel, none of the other processes (segments) would be necessary.

The illustration above also highlights that product and information typically flows in opposite directions, which leads to the possibility of **bullwhip** if left unchecked. We'll save a detailed discussion for a later chapter, but in essence bullwhip refers to small (or large) increases (or decreases) in demand, which can lead to exponential impacts across an end-to-end supply chain if information isn't proactively communicated with supply chain partners.

© Ryan Fletcher/shutterstock.com

Supply chains don't just exist for businesses that make a physical product, they exist for services as well. Valvoline Instant Oil Change (VIOC) is a great example of a service provider that has a very sophisticated supply chain system. Most people think only of the operational steps of visiting a VIOC location: a service tech checks the automobile's current oil level (as the starting reference point), drains the oil, refills the oil chamber to the exact specification as required by the automobile manufacturer, etc. But there's so much more to VIOC's supply chain! More people travel throughout the summer months, and because of this VIOC has a significant seasonal element. With peak summer demand, VIOC must plan for higher volumes and more frequent deliveries of oil and associated supplies (filters, wipers, bulbs, etc.) to the various locations. In addition, recycling of oils and fluids plays a huge role in supply chain environmental sustainability (see upcoming chapter).

Seasonality refers to those products and services for which a significant amount of annual demand occurs in a defined period—such as with patio sets sold predominantly during the summer months, and a disproportionally large percentage of LCD televisions sold between Black Friday (the day after Thanksgiving) and January (the Super Bowl and college football bowl games).

Valvoline Instant Oil Change provides a great example of the spectrum of goods and services within supply chain management. The term **spectrum** is used to classify (or categorize) something in terms of its position on a scale between two extreme or opposite points. Most "things" aren't necessarily one or the other, but a combination of both. In this instance, the oil itself is a tangible physical product, with the service element being that you don't have to perform the oil change yourself!

© Eric Glenn/shutterstock.com

Supply chains exist for nonprofit entities as well. A great example is **_humanitarian supply chains_**,[4] a relatively new term which describes those organizations—such as the Red Cross—that provide food, clothing, shelter, and medical supplies across the globe to communities in urgent need. Think of all the processes from collecting the various supplies and resources—everything from milk formula for infants to insulin for diabetics—to physically positioning (moving) those resources along with healthcare professionals and volunteers into areas where infrastructure (e.g., roads, airports, hospitals, power grids, etc.) may have been heavily damaged. Humanitarian supply chains highlight the importance of collaborative planning across various providers and the urgency with which decisions must be made and operationalized.

© Sergey Kohl/shutterstock.com

---

[4] Torabi, S. A., Shokr, I., Tofighi, S., & Heydari, J. (2018). Integrated relief pre-positioning and procurement planning in humanitarian supply chains. *Transportation Research Part E: Logistics and Transportation Review, 113*, 123–146.

Many people mistakenly think that a nonprofit organization is one that continuously operates with a financial loss. In short, nonprofit does <u>not</u> mean "for loss." In fact, no organization can operate with financial losses indefinitely. A nonprofit organization is one in which any residual (remaining) income—above the cost of providing the actual good and/or service for their specific mission—is used toward enhancing the ability to provide more goods and/or services in the future, as opposed to being distributed as profits to individual owners.

A hospital is a great example of a nonprofit organization—and they have supply chain systems, processes, and organizations, too. The ability to have the right equipment and supplies in a healthcare facility is often the difference between life and death. Healthcare facilities have missions, strategies, suppliers, inventory, and critical timelines like other organizations. Many leading hospitals are now placing a heightened role on supply chain as a way of enhancing and expanding their respective missions.

Supply chain management has become a major concern of healthcare providers as well, further exacerbated by many medical drugs and equipment coming from other countries in which production interruptions and unloading of cargo ships have become major issues. Reid Jones, CEO of UAB Medicine (Birmingham, AL.),[5] shares "we are seeing COVID-19-related manufacturing disruptions in some Asian countries that produce many of the everyday items we use in the healthcare setting. We also have pressure on the trucking industry in this country due to the increase in e-commerce over the past two years." As such many healthcare organizations are investing in new methods for monitoring global events that have the potential for impacting supply chain continuity.

© Evellean/shutterstock.com

---

5   Gooch, K. & Gonzalez, G. (2021, November 2). Supply chain issues are here to stay: health leaders share predictions, strategies. *Becker's Hospital Review.* https://www.beckershospitalreview.com/hospital-management-administration/supply-chain-issues-are-here-to-stay-health-leaders-share-predictions-strategies.html

Supply chain management is all around us in ways we rarely stop to think about. The coronavirus pandemic highlighted the importance of integrated supply chain processes and collaboration. The COVID-19 vaccine has a very complicated end-to-end supply chain with multiple companies involved in the production process, further complicated by requirements for the vaccine to be transported at extremely cold temperatures (***cold chain***) to prevent spoilage, as well as short time frames in which the vaccine can be used before its biological effectiveness expires. The pandemic highlighted the complexities of the ***last mile***, meaning that after all the planning that goes into making the vaccine, getting the vaccine effectively and efficiently into the hands of healthcare heroes in big cities and small towns across the globe is still a major challenge.

© Fit Ztudio/shutterstock.com

Now we're ready to dive much deeper into the wonderful world of supply chain management. In the following chapters, you'll learn much more about supply chain organizations, strategy, environmental sustainability, analytics, and project management, among many other things. Let's learn <u>and</u> have fun… it's OK to do both!

Supply Chain Organizations

In supply chain we have professionals—individuals and dynamic teams—who perform hundreds, if not thousands, of different tasks—from strategically (long-term) planning five-year capacity needs to operationally (daily) loading trucks and processing shipments. No supply chain employee can do "everything," but all supply chain employees do "something" that, collectively, enables products and services to be positioned and sold in the marketplace.

It is important to understand how supply chain fits into an overall organization. A business organization is comprised of different functions, ideally supporting each other to accomplish the overall goals and objectives of the business (see the upcoming *Strategy* chapter). The relationship and reporting structure of these interrelated functions is often displayed in an **organizational chart** (or "org chart" for short).

For a large multinational company, the top supply chain executive is often referred to as the **Chief Supply Chain Officer** (CSCO), or sometimes Chief Supply Officer (CSO). This role typically reports directly to the Chief Executive Officer (CEO) of the company, and generally has oversight for the entire supply chain function. Below is a highly simplified organizational chart detailing a typical layout of a multinational company. For illustrative purposes, Inventory Management is shown as a Planning function, and further categorized by two sub-departments—Raw Materials and Finished Goods.

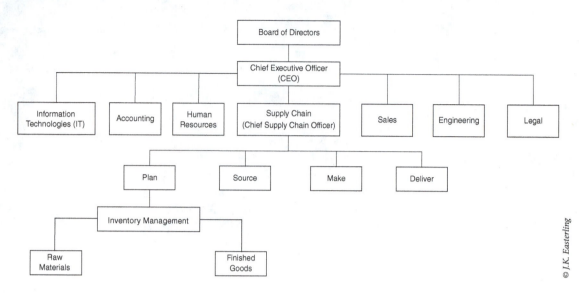

© J.K. Easterling

Organizational charts can be complicated, and include a combination of functions, tiers, reporting structures, geographies, and individual names. Some companies are highly secretive about their organizational structures for reasons such as discouraging rival companies (competitors) from recruiting key employees or <u>deemphasizing</u> the traditional sense of ***employees working to serve top management***.

Many companies now prefer an ***inverted organizational structure*** where the primary focus is on customers, and the role of senior managers is to ensure that workers (employees) have everything they need (e.g., safe working conditions and the necessary tools and training) to meet and exceed customer needs. This type of management style is often referred as ***servant leadership***, and in essence highlights that ***top management works to serve employees and customers***.

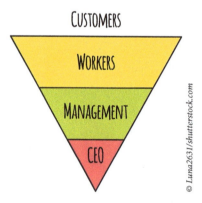

© Luna2631/shutterstock.com

Regardless of the complexity, simplicity, or even the absence of a formal reporting structure, supply chain is clearly an essential function within a larger multi-disciplined (e.g., accounting, sales, human resources) organization. ***Supply chain's overall role (in the context of a much larger organization) can be defined by one simple statement: to effectively manage supply and demand.*** While the statement is *simple*, the work is quite *complex*, and as such, there is a need for effective talent management.

It's important to note that supply chain <u>teams</u> are comprised of <u>individuals</u>, and certain skillsets and traits are highly desirable. Supply chain is an extremely dynamic field, as it engages heavily with other internal functions (departments), as well as externally with customers (downstream) and suppliers (upstream). On any given day, one or more of the following activities could (and probably will) happen: a supplier could be late (or early) with a delivery of raw materials, customer demand may dramatically increase (or decrease), a piece of equipment on an assembly line could fail, there may be a quality issue (either internally or externally), a shipment of finished goods crossing international borders could be held for inspection, an inventory discrepancy may exist—and at least a hundred other possibilities.

Individuals and teams that thrive in a fast-paced and ever-changing environment are in great demand by every supply chain organization. Other desirable traits include the ability to communicate effectively with others—both internally and externally, as well as orally and in writing—and an ability and willingness to collaboratively work with colleagues in other parts of the organization. Finally, great attention to detail is required, as many other functions of the organization (e.g., sales, accounting) are highly dependent upon the supply chain function. In fact, accounting and supply chain professionals have lots of similar tasks; accountants typically assess product (or service) movements in terms of <u>dollars</u>, whereas supply chain professionals usually refer to <u>units</u>—only the unit of measure differs.

Many colleges and universities now have formal degree programs in supply chain management. Many community colleges now offer two-year associate degrees providing training and pathways for entry-level supply chain roles. For those seeking advanced degrees, master's and doctoral degrees in supply chain management are available. Most large companies now offer forms of tuition assistance to support employees pursuing supply chain tracks, though typically with a required formal commitment by the employee to remain with the company for an extended period upon program completion (a "payback" of sorts). Many colleges and universities with specialized supply chain programs are now recruiting more minority students to help bridge an industry gap.

Many states are now launching vocational tracks in supply chain to help prepare secondary (i.e., high school) students for entry-level supply chain roles such as inventory analyst, warehouse attendant, shipping clerk, purchasing assistant, and material planner. It's essential that supply chain vocational tracks also include coursework across the entire SCOR Model to ensure that graduates have a foundational understanding of the integrated nature of supply chain operations. The quote below appropriately highlights the importance of having multiple tiers of supply chain programs—from colleges and universities to high schools—using a baseball analogy.

Gonzales shares that while there are various universities offering supply chain degree programs, there needs to be additional options (such as high school and community college programs) for those pursuing entry-level roles "where young students can explore their interest in the field and begin developing their knowledge and skills in balancing supply with demand, in making tradeoff decisions between inventory and transportation costs, in resolving issues and exploring opportunities with suppliers and customers." (Gonzalez)[6]

As with most fields of employment, there are also professional associations for individuals working in supply chain roles. Two that are widely known and highly regarded are the Association for Supply Chain Management (ASCM)[7] and the Institute for Supply Management (ISM),[8] which offer membership, training, and networking opportunities at the local, state, and national levels. Additionally, these associations offer optional programs leading to professional certifications, which are highly desired by companies of all sizes. Most professional certification programs require a combination of experience plus successful completion of a series of tests. Many companies provide financial support to help offset the cost of completing the qualifying tests. Once a certification is earned, it can be renewed by earning Continuing Professional Education (CPE) points by attending periodic meetings hosted by local chapters.

Professional Development Pays Off

This year's data continues to show that employers value those who seek continuing education. A supply chain professional with at least one credential can expect a 17% higher salary than those without. Those with two or more credentials enjoy an even larger gain, at 46% more than the median salary.

Salary by number of certifications

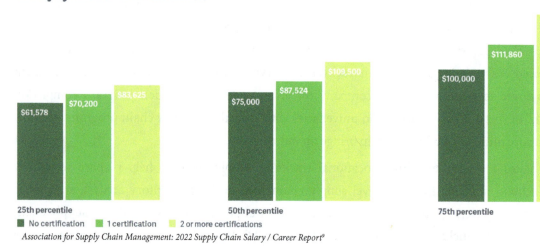

Association for Supply Chain Management: 2022 Supply Chain Salary / Career Report[9]

Copyright © ASCM 2022. Reprinted by permission.

---

6 Gonzalez, A. (2011). *Farm system for supply chain and logistics: Preparing the next generation of leaders.* https://talkinglogistics.com/2011/03/02/farm-system-supply-chain-preparing-next-generation-leaders/
7 Association for Supply Chain Management. (n.d.). *About ASCM.* https://www.ascm.org/
8 Institute for Supply Management. (n.d.). https://www.ismworld.org/
9 Association for Supply Chain Management (n.d.). *2022 Supply chain Salary and Career Report.* Pg. 20.

As with other functions, top supply chain managers must focus heavily on **talent management**. Talent management includes not only recruiting qualified employees, but also retaining, training, assessing, and developing employees for future growth.

Recruiting supply chain talent can be accomplished in a variety of ways. Many companies now recruit entry-level talent from college and university programs specializing in supply chain management. Many companies also offer college internship opportunities whereby students majoring in supply chain management gain valuable job experience while working part time. Most multinational companies now have "supply chain jobs" as a search criterion on their respective websites. For more experienced professionals, there are a growing number of **boutique recruiting agencies** that specialize in identifying senior and executive supply chain roles for select industries and companies.

© Nadya_Art/shutterstock.com

After a job offer has been extended to a prospective candidate, a negotiation usually commences in terms of salary and benefits. Supply chain professionals command heavy salaries (near the top of all business fields), especially those with considerable experience and a history of documented accomplishments. Many candidates receive incentives such as company stock, which typically vests over a specific time frame (e.g., three years). Some candidates negotiate up-front signing bonuses and/or a commitment for the employer to pay for professional certifications, additional schooling, more vacation time, etc. Once a candidate accepts a job offer, the process of **onboarding** begins, which typically involves formally welcoming and introducing the new employee, providing safety training, and completing any remaining employment paperwork.

Supply Chain Salaries

Supply chain salaries are up from 2020, with median total compensation increasing by 12% to $96,000 (including additional compensation). Overall, supply chain salaries ranged from $56,000 to $185,000 annually. Additional cash compensation includes cash bonus, profit sharing, incentive pay and overtime pay.

Additional Compensation

Nearly three-fourths (71%) of respondents earned at least one form of additional compensation, ranging from $3,000 to as high as $16,000. The median additional compensation was $8,000.

Additional forms of compensation received

60% Cash bonus   **13%** Profit sharing   **8%** Incentive pay   **7%** Overtime pay

Association for Supply Chain Management: 2022 Supply Chain Salary / Career Report[10]

    Upon completing the onboarding process, a new employee is generally assigned specific objectives, which of course should align with and enable the organization's overall goals and strategy (see the upcoming *Strategy* chapter). Every supply chain employee at every level should have MBOs (***Management by Objectives***)—a process in which the employee and supervisor <u>proactively</u> communicate and evaluate specific objectives on a recurring basis to ensure that progress is being made. MBOs help reduce vagueness around job responsibilities and expectations.

© Trueffelpix/shutterstock.com

---

[10] Association for Supply Chain Management (n.d.). *2022 Supply Chain Salary and Career Report*. Pg. 5.

As part of the overall Talent Management process, progressive companies have formal succession plans for key positions. A **succession plan** is a process whereby the status of the incumbent employee is listed, as well as projected replacements and expected timing of status changes. Per the illustration below, the incumbent (current) Supply Chain Manager is expected to be in his role for another 12–18 months before moving into an international role. Then, the current Planning Supervisor is expected to move into the role of Supply Chain Manager, and the Senior Logistician is expected to move into the role of Planning Supervisor. In essence, a succession plan shows the **domino effect** of people moves within a department or overall organization.

Succession Plan

Position: *Supply Chain Manager*

	Name	Current Position	Status	Targeted Replacement
1	Randy Miller	Incumbent	Probable international assignment within next 12-18 months	Blake Thompson
2	Blake Thompson	Planning Supervisor	Ready Now	Teresa Smith
3	Teresa Smith	Senior Logistician	Currently in 2-year Supply Chain Management / Masters degree program	Jenny Liu

© J.K. Easterling

Another key aspect of supply chain talent management is an **annual review**, which typically includes three essential pieces of information: the overall employee rating, current year achievements, and a development plan for ongoing growth. Most companies have an annual rating system for employees as part of the overall talent management process. Let's review the five typical categories of employee evaluation (note: companies use various terms for these categories).

- **High Potential (Hi-Po)** rating is generally reserved for those employees who top management perceives as having the potential to advance at least two levels within the company; for example, a Supply Chain Supervisor who is projected to become Planning Manager and eventually Supply Chain Director. High potential employees may be assigned a "coach" (mentor) and are often included in select training plans in areas such as leadership, managing global teams, and understanding diversity and inclusion. Generally, only about 15 percent of employees receive this rating.

- **Valued Contributor (VC)** rating is the largest rating category and includes employees who fully meet their respective job duties and MBOs. These employees, however, are not expected to advance significantly beyond their current roles. Generally, about 60 percent of employees receive this rating.

- **Developing** is the rating category for employees who are still progressing in terms of mastering their assigned role. Examples include an employee who just moved into a new lateral role (same overall level but new job responsibilities, perhaps in another area within supply chain), as well as an employee who just moved into a supervisory role from an individual contributor role and whose effectiveness is not yet known. Employees in this category may need extra coaching and mentoring. Generally, 10–15% percent of employees receive this rating.

- **Concern** is a rating category for employees who management perceives as having major issues that could lead to a different assignment, a required intervention, or possible termination. *Concern* does not necessarily imply that someone is a *bad* employee—and it certainly doesn't imply that an employee with a concern rating is a bad *person*. Rather, it may imply that an employee with a concern rating is one whose unique skillset is not a good fit in a particular role. It could also imply that team chemistry causes an employee to act or behave in a particularly undesirable way that wasn't observed in prior roles. Furthermore, it could suggest the employee has an urgent developmental need that needs immediate attention (for example, diversity training). Usually less than 10 percent of employees receive this rating.

- **Unknown** is generally reserved for those employees too new to the organization or role for their performance to be assessed. For example, a new employee who just graduated college and has been with the company a short period of time. Or an employee who transferred in from a different division or location. Generally, less than 5 percent of employees are rated as unknown, and an employee usually only receives this rating for one year.

It's important to note that ratings are usually applied as part of an annual performance review. However, it's not uncommon for an employee's rating to change over time. In fact, this is the perfect transition to discussing development plans. A ***development plan*** is a detailed listing of specific actions to either overcome a weakness or to strengthen an existing skillset. It's never enough to simply list developmental needs; rather, an action plan including timing and location are always needed. Below is an example of an annual performance review detailing the employee's overall rating and accomplishments for the past year, as well as a development plan, which includes timing.

Annual Performance Review		
Name: Shiloh DeVore **Title:** Purchasing Supervisor **Overall employee rating:** High Potential		
Current Year Achievements		
1 Led Purchasing Department to record annual cost reductions ($3 million) 2 Began monthly recognition program for team members reaching individual objectives 3 Completed Supply Chain professional certification program 4 Ensured every team member completed Ethics program for supplier negotiations		
Development Plan	**Timing**	**How / Where**
1 Attend "Future Global Leaders" program for Hi-Po employees	Quarter 1	Corporate training (Japan)
2 Improve public speaking / presentation skills	Quarter 2	Local community college course
3 Cross-train in Logistics Department	2nd half of year	Job rotation program (internal)

© J.K. Easterling

Those individuals reaching executive levels of supply chain management typically have considerable experience across multiple SCOR pillars, which enables having a wider perspective to draw upon for decision making. As such, individuals desiring to become senior supply chain managers and executives often seek experience in planning, sourcing, logistics, operations, etc.; many companies have **rotational programs** whereby designated employees (typically High Potential) spend 9–12 months in one role before transitioning to another. These rotational programs provide invaluable insight into how the various SCOR pillars are integrated.

In addition to experience across various functions, select supply chain employees—especially those working for large multinational companies—may be chosen for international assignments, which also provides more insight and perspective on cultures, values, and beliefs in other countries. An **expatriate** is an employee who works outside their home country—generally for longer than one year—on behalf of their employer. Being chosen for an international assignment is a great honor, and typically comes after many years of documented achievements—not just in driving business results, but also in engaging coworkers in a collaborative and positive manner. The ability and willingness to contribute to a **Positive Work Environment (PWE)** is very important for supply chain professionals, especially in international roles.

© MOLPIX/shutterstock.com

Just like an organization has specific goals and an associated strategy (i.e., plan) for success, each employee should have a long-term goal(s) and strategy as well. The path taken—a job or a career—is ultimately the responsibility of the EMPLOYEE. It's important to note that a **career** and a **job** are not the same thing, though many people mistakenly use the words interchangeably. A job infers work that doesn't differ dramatically over time and offers limited opportunities for growth. A career, however, infers more responsibilities, a wider sphere of influence, advancement opportunities, and higher levels of compensation. Hence the need to proactively plan for professional certifications, a possible advanced degree, experience across various functional areas, ownership of developmental needs, and above all else, a proven track record of consistently exceeding objectives (MBOs).

"Don't make excuses…find solutions"

In every departmental function (including supply chain) there are essentially two types of employees: those who <u>report</u> results, and those who <u>drive</u> performance. Employees who report results are reactive, simply looking at what happened in some time period (for example last month) and stating the results; these types of employees mostly stay in entry-level type roles throughout their career or cap out at low levels of management. Conversely, those employees who drive performance exhibit a proactive mentality in continuously assessing options and implementing ideas and programs in the pursuit of even higher levels of performance.

Strategy is one of the most important concepts in the business world, though most people mistakenly use the terms *strategy* and *goal* interchangeably. To simplify, a **strategy** is a fancy word for a plan—an action (or set of actions) an organization takes to accomplish a specific goal(s). In other words, a **goal** is what an organization seeks to accomplish, whereas a strategy is the action(s) an organization takes to achieve its goal(s). As you can now see, a goal and a strategy then—as we often say in business—are "*related but not the same thing.*"

- **Goal:** <u>what</u> an organization wants to achieve
- **Strategy:** <u>how</u> an organization plans to achieve a specific goal(s)

"A goal without a plan [strategy] is a wish"

Understanding a firm's mission and vision are essential for formulating strategy at all levels—corporate, business, and functional. A **mission statement** details why an organization or business exists (i.e., its purpose) and the current market it's attempting to serve, whereas a **vision statement** is more aspirational and future-oriented. Understanding a company's mission (i.e., *where we are now*) and vision (i.e., *where we're trying to go*) are essential for formulating strategy.

Let's dive into the three levels of strategy: corporate, business, and functional. **Corporate strategy** is conducted at the very highest level of the organization. Top <u>internal</u> leaders of the organization (e.g., Chief Executive Officer, President, Chief Financial Officer), along with the Board of Directors (which also includes <u>external</u> representation), decide where the organization is going to allocate its **scarce** (limited) resources. External members of the Board of Directors serve in various roles, including bringing an independent and outside perspective, providing oversight of the CEO and executive team, and representing shareholder interests (in companies publicly traded in the stock market).

Many people naively think large multinational organizations are unlimited in terms of resources, such as cash and the ability to borrow money, but that's simply not true. As with individuals, large organizations have constraints, too. In other words, strategic decisions must be made regarding where to allocate an organization's scarce resources. Corporate strategy, then, defines the industry(s) *where* an organization competes. A large corporation could compete exclusively in a singular industry or in many different industries.

The term **conglomerate** refers to an organization that competes in many different (often unrelated) industries. The term **strategic business unit (SBU)** is often used to describe a specific business unit within a larger overall company. For example, suppose a conglomerate competes in the following six industries: oil and gas, automotive, healthcare, environmental, consulting, and aeronautics. The leaders of <u>each</u> respective strategic business unit must decide how they're going to compete against other competitors in each unique industry.

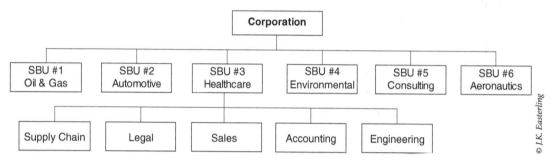

Business strategy defines **how** an SBU competes in its unique industry, either through **price leadership** or some form of **differentiation**. For any product or service, there are value-oriented customers (those seeking low prices) and highly discerning customers (those seeking a product or service with some differentiating aspect). Organizations **differentiate** themselves from competitors to highlight product or service uniqueness in various ways. Approaches to differentiation include product/service design, convenience, superior quality, responsiveness, innovation, flexibility, or exceptional customer service, among others. Some example organizations are listed below:

- **Carhartt:** superior quality
- **Disney Resorts:** exceptional customer service
- **Valvoline Instant Oil Change:** convenience
- **Apple:** innovation
- **IKEA:** product/service design
- **Amazon:** responsiveness
- **Burger King:** flexibility ("have it your way")

Organizations that differentiate their products (or services) tend to be able to charge a **price premium**, meaning customers recognize and are willing to pay more because of some perceived higher value, which is often referred to as **value proposition** ("value prop"). Price leadership implies that an organization strives to sell its product (or service) at a lower price than competitors. When a firm competes on price, the product (or service) is often a **commodity**, meaning there are no discernable product (or service) attributes (i.e., the product/service is **generic**).

In a conglomerate, each SBU is periodically assessed for both <u>relative</u> market share and market growth rate to help guide the organization toward decisions around future investments or possible **divesture,** which refers to selling ("*spinning off*") an SBU to generate cash for investing in higher growth areas. **Market growth rate** is future-oriented and represents how the overall market is expected to grow over time, usually expressed in terms of number of units or customers. **Market share**, on the other hand, is present-time oriented and represents the current share relative to the overall existing market. By the way, **relative** is a very important word—it means that its **directionally correct** but likely has a degree of error, as companies tend to naively overstate their market share. For example, when a company states a specific SBU has 60-percent market share, it means the *estimated* market share is 60 percent based on the best available (and often most optimistic) information. Market share is a directional measure at best.

SBUs need to be periodically assessed in terms of overall competitiveness, and this is often done using the highly valuable Boston Consulting Group (BCG) Matrix.[11] As per the illustration below, there are two axes: **relative market share** on the horizontal axis, and **market growth rate** on the vertical axis. The BCG Matrix is divided into four quadrants:

- **Dog**: SBUs that have both low market share and low market growth rate, and are candidates for divesting to raise capital (generate cash from the sale) to reinvest in faster growing SBUs.

- **Cash Cow**: SBUs that have high market share and low market growth rate, which generally refers to an industry that is maturing (minimal future growth), yet one that still generates significant cash flow.

- **Question Mark**: SBUs that have low market share and high market growth rate, which infers two things: (1) the industry is somewhat new with lots of growth potential; and/or (2) there's reason to believe market share can be substantially increased, perhaps by a new research and development initiative or different pricing strategy.

- **Stars**: SBUs that have high market share and high market growth rate. Obviously, the goal is to have more "Stars"—meaning business units with both high market share (current) and high market growth rate (future). These SBUs traditionally receive proportionally higher funding in expectation of higher future returns.

---

[11] Hambrick, D. C., MacMillan, I. C., & Day, D. L. (1982). Strategic attributes and performance in the BCG Matrix—a PIMS-based analysis of industrial product businesses. *Academy of Management Journal, 25*(3), 510–531.

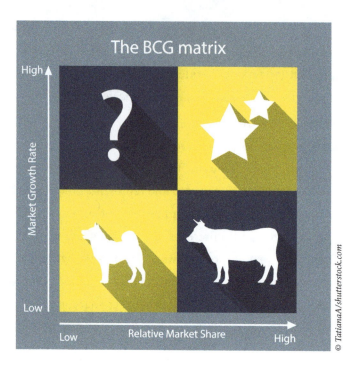

The BCG matrix

Market Growth Rate — High / Low
Relative Market Share — Low / High

© TatianaA/shutterstock.com

Organizations often perform a **SWOT analysis** to gauge competitive positioning with other companies. SWOT analysis is often done in combination with the BCG Matrix referenced earlier. SWOT analysis includes examining <u>internal</u> strengths and weaknesses, while assessing <u>external</u> opportunities and threats. Strengths and weaknesses are controlled by the company, and include variables such as intellectual property, patents, and talent acquisition and retention. Opportunities and threats cannot be completely controlled by the company, and include variables such as raw material pricing, global capacity constraints, and competitor research and development initiatives. Note that simply documenting SWOT elements is of little value. The real value comes from proactively developing actionable and executable plans based on the information obtained.

Every company in every industry has their own estimates on existing market share and future market growth potential. Obviously, every company can't be right. The key is intensive market research that has been vetted by various constituents—internal executive teams and outside consultants—complemented by a thorough SWOT analysis.

SWOT

STRENGTHS　　WEAKNESSES　　OPPORTUNITIES　　THREATS

© Trueffelpix/shutterstock.com

Let's now turn our focus to *functional strategy*. The word *functional* refers to the different departments within an organization: accounting, information technologies (IT), human resource management (HRM), engineering, legal, sales, and, of course, supply chain management. Employees working in each of those respective areas should be laser-focused, *aligning, enabling, and supporting* the organizational goals to be achieved—this is what's referred to as *strategic fit*—and it's one of the most important concepts in supply chain management. Strategic fit highlights the difference between "*doing things right*" and "*doing the right things*," meaning that each function should be taking <u>specific</u> actions that help the organization achieve its <u>specific</u> goals.

If, for example, an organization seeks to differentiate by superior quality, then all departments—including all supply chain pillars—should be focused on superior quality as well. Conversely, if an organization competes on price leadership, then the supply chain function should be focused on price leadership, too. Strategic fit, then, means the actions taken by a functional department—supply chain management in this example—*aligns, enables, and supports* a specific organizational goal to be achieved.

We can use a simple example to illustrate strategic fit. Assume that an organization has a goal of reducing incoming quality defects, which coincidently, is impacted by the actions (or inactions) of many different functional areas. To be actionable, the goal should be expressed in a manner consistent with the SMART[12] concept and written in the following manner: *Reduce incoming quality defects by 10 percent compared to last year's results before the start of the next fiscal year.* What's special about this goal? Well, I'm glad you asked. The goal is now:

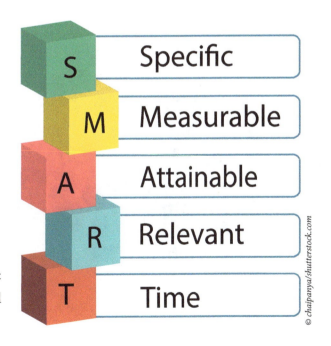

© chaipanya/shutterstock.com

- **S**: clear, concise, and tangible in terms of a <u>specific</u> goal the organization wants to accomplish (reduce quality defects)
- **M**: <u>measurable</u> in terms of quantifying the goal (reduce defects by 10 percent)
- **A**: <u>attainable</u> in terms of a realistic goal and baseline (compared to last year's results)
- **R**: <u>relevant</u> in terms of helping the organization compete—especially if the organization competes using a strategy of superior quality (more on this soon)
- **T**: <u>time-based</u> or stated in terms of a specific <u>timeframe</u> (before the start of the next fiscal year)

---

[12] Latham, G. P. (2003). Goal setting: a five-step approach to behavior change. *Organizational Dynamics, 32*(3), 309–318.

Most organizational goals cannot be achieved in terms of a singular action, but rather require multiple actions. To illustrate strategic fit, the supply chain functional strategy (the "*how*") would likely include the elements below in the effort of reducing incoming quality defects:

1. Provide clearly defined **specifications** to suppliers on all purchased items.

2. Conduct periodic **supplier audits** to evaluate process capabilities.

3. Perform **incoming inspection** on all supplier deliveries to <u>proactively</u> identify incoming defects.

4. Implement **periodic scorecards** to provide suppliers with timely feedback for purposes of continuous improvement ("*kaizen*").

5. Require **corrective actions** from suppliers for defective products.

Are these the only functional actions the supply chain function could take to help the overall organization achieve its goal? Of course not! This example is simply meant to illustrate specific actions taken by the supply chain function, which directly align, enable, and support a specific organizational goal to make it achievable.

Strategy is a highly complicated area, and in fact, most multinational companies have a Chief Strategy Officer (typically reporting directly to the CEO) who leads overall efforts across the entire corporation. Strategic business units frequently have strategy directors and managers who help develop aligned goals across the various functional departments.

© Phattana Stock/Shutterstock.com

Global Supply Chains

Chapter 4

Organizations often pursue international strategies to increase share in an existing market or to launch a product or service into a new market. There are four primary ways in which companies expand internationally, each with major supply chain implications. Let's review the four approaches in detail.

Exporting occurs when a product is made domestically and shipped directly into other countries. This approach to international expansion provides an ability to test product reception in the new market without fully committing to major investments. Exporting also allows a company to keep internal control over key processes such as production, quality, and intellectual property (IP). However, shipping products over longer distances enables more opportunities for damage, theft, and delay. Great proficiency in processing shipments across international borders is required to avoid products being held by Customs due to incorrect and/or incomplete paperwork. Some countries specify unique packaging requirements, such as plastic containers (instead of wood) or heat-treated wood pallets to reduce the likelihood of pest infestations.

Exporting is also challenging in regards to responding quickly to increases in customer demand, and often requires the use of expedited transportation (e.g., an emergency air shipment), which greatly increases overall costs. Formal *trade agreements* often exist between countries to encourage trade, and may include expedited processing of shipments, reduced duties and tariffs (fees for product crossing international borders), and heightened protection of intellectual property.

Joint ventures (JVs) occur when two (or more) companies contractually agree to form an entity to provide a product (or service) in a specific country. Joint ventures are typically characterized by each company having a skill(s) or asset(s) the other company doesn't. For example, one company may have a significant amount of cash to invest but a limited research and development (R&D) portfolio, whereas another company may have a robust R&D portfolio but limited cash; in other words, joint ventures often highlight *complementary strengths*. There is no requirement that joint ventures be equally owned (i.e., 50/50). In fact, when an entity is equally owned, potential disagreements can lead to major roadblocks and stagnation in terms of decision making. Joint ventures are tightly structured with formal timelines (often 7–10 years with options for renewal), and typically are composed of a board of directors with top executive representation from both companies. Joint venture agreements should explicitly state how profits (or losses) will be shared, and whether profits will be returned to each party or reinvested. Joint venture agreements should also document specific supply chain roles and responsibilities in terms of planning, sourcing, packaging, delivery, etc.

Licensing is an approach where a company enters into a formal agreement to allow another company to make and sell its products (or services) in return for a set fee or a percentage of profits. The major advantage to this approach is lower up-front investment when stepping into a foreign market. However, there are substantial risks with licensing in terms of IP disclosure, as well as lower control over production, quality, and customer service.

Licensing is often used with **contract manufacturers** (CMs), which are companies that don't necessarily make and sell their own products, but rather focus on making products or providing services for other companies. In this sense, licensing is essentially outsourcing production to another company. Licensing agreements should only be entered into with sound advice from legal counsel and the presence of non-disclosure agreements (NDAs). Many companies use licensing agreements to "test the waters" for a predefined period (e.g., 12–24 months) to see if the product will be successful in the new international market, and then may proceed to another form of expansion (such as a joint venture or direct ownership).

Direct ownership occurs when a company decides to purchase (or lease) property in a foreign country and set up independent operations. This approach entails great risk in terms of investment and requires high levels of commitment and resources. Advantages include maintaining oversight of production, quality, and IP, and having closer access and more direct engagement with customers in the new market. In lesser-developed countries, a typical challenge is getting approval from governmental agencies to begin construction and start production. **Grease payments** is a term used to describe payments to governmental officials to ease restrictions or expedite paperwork/applications (these types of illicit payments are highly frowned upon). There's often a cultural element as well that can be challenging when bringing management styles into a country that may have different values and beliefs.

From a supply chain perspective, direct ownership enables full control over production, supplier selection, transportation, and customer deliveries. Great care must be taken to understand the expected volume and variety of products in the new market, as strategic decisions are not easily changed. Setting up a new facility in a domestic market is rather challenging; setting up a new facility in a foreign country is exponentially more difficult given so many unknown decision points.

It's important to note that approaches to international expansion may change over time based on market maturity, product acceptance, financial conditions, competitive pressures, IP changes, etc. For example, a particular company might elect to start with exporting goods into a new market and may or may not evolve

over time to joint venture, licensing, or direct ownership. In short, there's not a "one size fits most" approach that applies to all companies. In fact, this topic of international expansion perfectly highlights the dynamic aspect of business and how plans evolve over time as inputs (factors) change.

International expansion isn't the only "global" aspect of supply chain management. Multinational companies typically have manufacturing, sourcing, logistics, and planning teams throughout the regions they serve. Corning Incorporated, one of America's oldest (founded in 1851) and most respected companies, has over 61,000 employees worldwide across more than 30 countries with over 150 global locations. Corning has global supply chain offices strategically located to support businesses in various regions. For example, Corning's supply chain office in Singapore supports Corning's business units operating in Southeast Asia, whereas their supply chain office in Switzerland supports business units throughout Europe.

The sourcing pillar often has a heavy global aspect, as most companies source products and services across many countries. In fact, many companies have **international procurement offices (IPOs)** to manage and coordinate global purchases. Having IPOs strategically placed helps with many aspects of supply chain management, including the ability to respond quickly when supplier issues arise. Most IPOs have a team that focuses on **Social Responsibility Audits (SRAs)**, which is an approach to ensuring suppliers act in ways that reflect the buying company's values and beliefs in order to avoid reputational damage.[13] Child labor, poor safety conditions, lack of rest periods, hostile work environments, excessive overtime, and unreasonable output expectations are all examples of social responsibility concerns.

SRAs are a form of limiting what is often referred to as "**exporting smokestacks**," meaning moving processes to countries (often underdeveloped countries) where worker safety and environmental concerns are less prevalent. Most companies now recognize that global suppliers are simply an extension of the organization, and that supplier actions, policies, and procedures should directly reflect the buying firm's values and beliefs.

---

[13] Tekin, E. K., Ertürk, A., & Tozan, H. (2015). Corporate social responsibility in supply chains. *Applications of Contemporary Management Approaches in Supply Chains*, 1–12.

Forecasting

Organizations use forecasting tools and techniques as part of their managerial and budgetary processes. A ***forecast*** is in essence a prediction, projection, or estimation about the future based on underlying assumptions. Forecasts generally assume underlying ***causal*** *factors*, meaning the assumptions (market size, market share, prior sales history, etc.) that were relevant in the past are likely to be relevant going forward. Many people correctly associate "sales" with forecasting, and indeed sales forecasting is a common task for most companies. However, many variables can be forecasted, such as labor needs, raw materials usage, expected defects, and earnings per share (EPS). In fact, every functional department uses forecasting tools and techniques as part of their specific operational, tactical, and strategic plans.

There are many different types of forecasting models, but they are categorized into two major areas: quantitative and qualitative. Quantitative models, as the name implies, are more objective and primarily use mathematical data as the major input. Qualitative models, conversely, are more subjective and rely more on executive opinion, judgment, and experience. So, which is best? Quantitative <u>and</u> qualitative techniques should be combined for any model to provide more depth and perspective. Forecasting models vary by cost, accuracy, future time horizon, and other factors. Most large companies have multi-million dollar forecasting systems, some of which are custom built for a unique business or industry.

© Sergey Nivens/shutterstock.com

Raw material shortages, global production capacity, and fluctuating prices are concerns for companies of all sizes. Therefore, functional leaders must be concerned with forecasting from both financial and supply chain operational perspectives. External customers typically commit to firm orders for short periods of time (possibly the next 3–4 weeks), whereas companies may need to commit to upstream suppliers for longer time periods (3–6+ months) for items or services that are unique.

Forecasting assumptions (inputs) are represented by a wide range of internal and external variables. Internal assumptions can include market share, production capacity, availability of raw materials, pricing strategy, etc. External assumptions can include overall market size, consumer discretionary income, overall employment outlook, borrowing (interest) rates, presence of a national and/or global health pandemic, strength of competitors, etc.

© Natee Meepian/shutterstock.com

Efforts should be made to measure and improve forecast accuracy due to the impact on supply chain performance. Therefore, organizations should seek to have higher alignment between actual performance and forecast. The difference between what was forecasted for any period and what occurred is referred to as **_forecast deviation_** (sometimes called forecast error). Firms measure forecast accuracy using two primary tools: Mean Absolute Deviation (MAD) and Mean Absolute Percentage Error (MAPE). MAD is an approach to measuring forecast accuracy by calculating the average number of deviations in terms of _units_. MAPE is an approach to measuring forecast accuracy by calculating the average number of deviations in terms of _percentage_. Note that MAD and MAPE use mathematical averages of the deviations to smooth out individual period random variation.

Below is an example of a typical forecast accuracy table. Period could be daily, weekly, quarterly, yearly, etc. In this instance, we have 10 years of historical data showing the volume forecasted for each respective period and what occurred. MAD is 112,944 (rounded to nearest whole number), meaning that on average this company has a forecast deviation of 112,944 units per year. MAPE helps with adding perspective in that while 112,944 seems like a big number (it is a BIG number!), the annualized average percentage forecast error is 4.51 percent. If this company has a forecast accuracy goal of 95 percent (meaning a 5 percent inaccuracy allowance), then the company would be achieving its goal, as 4.51 percent < 5 percent. And in fact, we see a favorable upward trend in forecast accuracy across the 10-year horizon (see column H).

A	B	C	D	E = C - D	F = absolute E	G = F/C	H = 100% - G
Period	Year	Units Sold (Actual)	Forecast (Plan)	Forecast Deviation (Actual - Forecast)	Absolute Error	Forecast Inaccuracy %	Forecast Accuracy
1	2012	1,975,800	1,850,542	125,258	125,258	6.34%	93.7%
2	2013	2,074,590	2,198,171	-123,581	123,581	5.96%	94.0%
3	2014	2,188,692	2,069,110	119,582	119,582	5.46%	94.5%
4	2015	2,317,825	2,433,812	-115,987	115,987	5.00%	95.0%
5	2016	2,456,895	2,347,313	109,582	109,582	4.46%	95.5%
6	2017	2,609,222	2,715,809	-106,587	106,587	4.09%	95.9%
7	2018	2,786,649	2,688,514	98,135	98,135	3.52%	96.5%
8	2019	2,981,715	3,076,872	-95,157	95,157	3.19%	96.8%
9	2020	3,196,398	3,076,816	119,582	119,582	3.74%	96.3%
10	2021	3,436,128	3,552,115	-115,987	115,987	3.38%	96.6%
				Totals for Period 1–10	1,129,438	45.14%	

Measure	Formula	Calculation
MAD	1,129,438 total absolute errors / 10 periods	112,944
MAPE	45.14% total % error / 10 periods	4.51%

Forecasting tools and techniques are commonly used across the various SCOR pillars, which is the perfect segue to our next chapter on *Supply Chain Integration*. An action in one area of supply chain—for example a three-month tactical finished goods production plan—leads to a forecast (projection) for packaging, warehousing, and transportation needs. In other words, packaging, warehousing, and transportation needs are dependent upon—or *derived* from—the finished goods production plan.

Supply Chain Integration

As with most aspects of supply chain, integration is not a simple task to achieve. Integration is necessary between the supply chain pillars (i.e., within each function) and between supply chain and other internal functions, as well as externally—both upstream (toward suppliers) and downstream (toward customers). This encompasses every department internally and adds several external companies to the conversation. In addition, all participants need to be able to communicate the information throughout their companies in a timely manner. This requires digital technology that will communicate across internal and external channels. This type of internal and external integration is often referred to as "*Enable*"—the sixth element of the SCOR Model. How can companies achieve this level of integration? Let's find out.

Sales and Operations Plan (S&OP) is a strategic process in which senior functional leaders (e.g., sales, operations, engineering, supply chains, etc.) meet on a recurring basis (typically at least once per month) to review the latest sales projections (the "demand plan") and the associated Ability to Supply (ATS) goods and services over an extended period—typically 12–18+ months. Decisions made in S&OP meetings focus more on <u>strategic issues</u>, such as long-term capacity needs, necessary equipment purchases, major repairs, timing of research and development (R&D) trials, the purchase of customer-unique packaging, etc. While multiple senior functional managers participate in S&OP meetings, the three primary functions are <u>S</u>ales, <u>O</u>perations, and <u>P</u>lanning (i.e., supply chain). Let's examine the overall process in more detail.

© dizain/shutterstock.com

The sales organization (sometimes called marketing or commercial) owns the relationship with external downstream customers and is responsible for sales projections (the demand plan), which is the starting point for all supply chain processes. Given the complexity of most companies, sales projections extending 12–18+ months is necessary. For example, some specialty factory equipment may have a two- to three-year lead time. Typically, the demand plan includes sales projections by month, customer, and product (or service) to provide management the necessary visibility to compare to previous forecasts. Below is an illustrative example of a basic 12-month demand plan. Remember that long-term demand plans are typically derived from both firm (committed) customer orders and forecasting techniques (reflect on the prior *Forecasting* chapter).

12-month Demand Plan (# of units)														
Customer	LTSA?	Internal Product ID	May	Jun	Jul	Aug	Sep	Oct	Nov	Dec	Jan	Feb	Mar	Apr
Johnson Co.	Yes	42795-A	13041	13237	13435	13637	13841	14049	14260	14473	14691	14911	15135	14885
Callihan & Co.	Yes	42795-A	7492	7642	7795	7951	8110	8272	8437	8606	8778	8954	9133	9315
Farris	No	42795-B	8492	8653	8818	8985	9156	9330	9507	9688	9872	10060	10251	10445
Bentley Brothers	No	81414-R	2393	2435	2477	2521	2565	2610	2656	2702	2749	2797	2846	2896
West Coast Inc.	Yes	81415-L	8942	9121	9303	9489	9679	9873	10070	10272	10477	10687	10900	11118
Coleman Inc.	No	7548778-PC	4711	4782	4853	4926	5000	5075	5151	5228	5307	5387	5467	5549
Estes	No	4320634-JA	3255	3314	3373	3434	3496	3559	3623	3688	3754	3822	3891	3961
Frank Industries	No	4320634-JA	4315	4380	4445	4512	4580	4648	4718	4789	4861	4934	5008	5083
Total Expected Demand			52641	53563	54500	55455	56427	57415	58422	59446	60489	61550	62630	63253

© J.K. Easterling

The sales team provides the demand plan to supply chain for a variety of different planning activities (reference the *Plan* chapter). Supply chain must **plan** for many things: capacity, production, raw materials, packaging, and transportation, just to name a few! The culmination of all these planning processes—and in direct response to the demand plan—is what's referred to as **Ability to Supply (ATS)**, more formally known as the supply plan.

As alluded to in the *Introduction to Supply Chain* chapter, supply (what our organization can deliver) and demand (what we project customers want) are never the same, especially beyond a very short time frame. Companies either have too much supply or not enough supply. Competitive pressures are continuous with rival companies implementing sales promotions and rolling out new and/or enhanced features to increase market share. As such, there's always a mismatch between supply and demand, which we refer to as supply constraints and demand constraints. Let's examine each.

A **supply constraint** occurs when demand exceeds supply, meaning a company doesn't have enough supply to meet the demand of all customers in some period (e.g., this month). During these periods, companies try to maximize supply capability by focusing heavily on productivity (output) and using slow-moving inventory. Tough business decisions must be made when there's not enough supply for all customers. Assume, for example, that at the end of April there are 5000 unit of inventory, with May production capacity/capability of 45,000 units, for a total May ability to supply of 50,000 units (which assumes keeping no safety stock). Reference back to the demand plan for May, which shows customers (combined) want 52,641 units, whereas ATS is only 50,000 units, or 95 percent of what's really needed. This challenge highlights what is referred to as **allocation**—a process of dividing what can be supplied relative to what customers want. What actions could be taken? One option would be to provide each customer 95 percent of their request, which is a <u>level allocation</u> across all customers. **Long-term supply agreements (LTSAs)** often exist with preferred customers, which in essence means those customers get 100 percent of what they ask for (within some predefined upper boundaries), and then the remaining balance is allocated to remaining customers. The table below highlights that Johnson Co., Callihan & Co., and West Coast Inc. are all LTSA customers, and as such get 100 percent of their requested volume. The five remaining customers are prorated based on other possible criteria (e.g., customer growth potential, pricing structure, future anticipated sales, etc.), with May planned shipments to all customers totaling 50,000 ATS. Again, this example and table is simplified for illustrative purposes.

Customer	LTSA?	Internal Product ID	May Request	May Planned Shipment	% Planned Fullfillment
Johnson Co.	**Yes**	42795-A	13041	13041	100%
Callihan & Co.	**Yes**	42795-A	7492	7492	100%
Farris	No	42795-B	8492	7767	91%
Bentley Brothers	No	81414-R	2393	2273	95%
West Coast Inc.	**Yes**	81415-L	8942	8942	100%
Coleman Inc.	No	7548778-PC	4711	4085	87%
Estes	No	4320634-JA	3255	2800	86%
Frank Industries	No	4320634-JA	4315	3600	83%
Total Expected Demand			**52641**	**50000**	

© J.K. Easterling

As the old saying goes, "a picture is worth a thousand words." Supply chain professionals frequently use tables, diagrams, graphs, and other illustrations to help communicate status and/or progress toward specific goals and objectives. The bar chart below shows the same information as the table above, albeit in a different format. Supply chain professionals must be able to process and communicate large amounts of information in a timely manner. We'll look at more examples in the upcoming *Analytics* chapter.

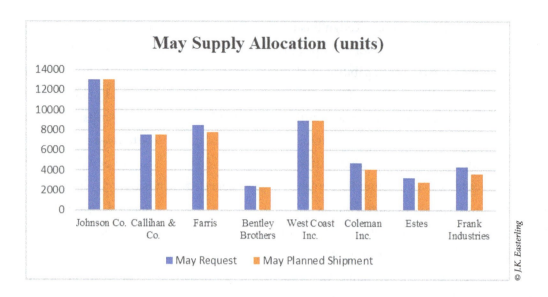

May Supply Allocation (units)

Chart showing May Request and May Planned Shipment by company:
- Johnson Co.
- Callihan & Co.
- Farris
- Bentley Brothers
- West Coast Inc.
- Coleman Inc.
- Estes
- Frank Industries

Legend: ■ May Request ■ May Planned Shipment

© J.K. Easterling

A ***demand constraint*** occurs when supply (ATS) capability exceeds customer demand, which infers inventory will be increasing unless offsetting adjustments are taken. In the short term, management may elect to strategically build inventory on certain products, focus on additional training for employees, perform preventive maintenance on equipment, or conduct R&D trials. Some companies may elect to incentivize customers to increase their orders by offering promotions or sales discounts. If a demand constraint exists for an extended period, management may elect to idle some processes, and could consider labor cuts, which is commonly referred to as ***reductions in force (RIFs)***.

In summary, the desired outcome of an S&OP process is a data-driven business plan that's followed by all functional departments for a specific period. Some executives use the phrase "singing from the same hymnal" to infer that all internal departments are working in an <u>integrated</u> manner on an agreed-upon plan. The S&OP process is typically refreshed each month with a new 12- to 18-month outlook. As such, S&OP isn't a one-time process, but rather an ongoing strategic process.

While S&OP focuses more strategically (long term), the need for integration and collaboration exists operationally (short term) and tactically (near term) as well. ***Enterprise Resource Planning (ERP)*** systems provide short- and near-term integration and collaboration by sharing business processes across various functions for real-time decision making. ERP uses systems, software, and technology to integrate internal functional departments to work collaboratively toward fulfilling shared objectives.

ERP — INVENTORY, FINANCIALS, HRM, PRODUCTION, SERVICE, PURCHASING, MRP

© Trueffelpix/shutterstock.com

Think about the two extreme points in supply chain planning: receiving of a customer order (beginning) and the fulfillment of a customer order (end). Sounds simple, right? The process is comprised of many steps, such as the sales team receiving and acknowledging the customer order; supply chain checking inventory records (finished goods, raw materials, packaging, etc.); operations preparing for actual production (checking specifications, calibrating equipment, etc.); quality preparing control charts; human resources ensuring the workforce is trained and prepared; and accounting making financial transactions, etc. Imagine the power of having all those internal departments working from a common plan in an integrated and collaborative manner—it's a lot like synchronized swimming. ERP systems drive higher overall organizational effectiveness at the operational and tactical levels, just as S&OP does this at the strategic level.

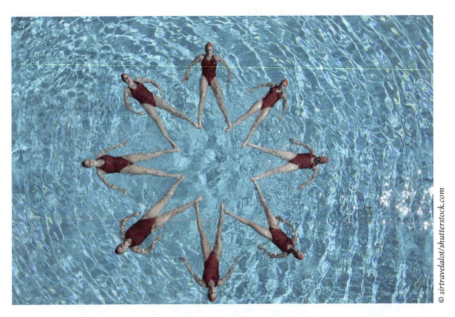

© sirtravelalot/shutterstock.com

Integration and collaboration don't just apply to internal operations. Rather, these processes apply externally as well—both upstream (toward suppliers) and downstream (toward customers). In fact, supply chain integration and collaboration should extend "*from your customer's customer to your supplier's supplier.*" One of the biggest changes over the past ~30 years is moving from treating external companies—particularly suppliers—as adversaries to treating them as partners. One way this can be accomplished is through establishment of a ***Collaborative Planning, Forecasting, and Replenishment (CPFR)*** program, a process that focuses on proactively sharing business plans and other essential information with upstream and downstream supply chain partners. Conceptually, the process is like the S&OP internal process, except CFPR is externally focused. Regardless, the intent is essentially the same, to proactively make data-based decisions that are shared across supply chain partners.

"Supply Chain collaboration should extend from your supplier's supplier to your customer's customer"

There's no defined "one way" to implement and run a CPFR process. Rather, the key point is sharing business plans that can be proactively used by upstream and downstream partners. For example, if downstream customer demand increases by 10 percent, then that same information should be proactively shared with upstream partners so that corresponding adjustments can be made accordingly. Without sharing business plans on a proactive basis, supply chain partners may experience the **bullwhip effect**, which describes situations where downstream changes (either increases or decreases), if not communicated properly, can have a devastating effect causing upstream companies to overreact (e.g., significantly changing staffing needs, production schedules, or inventory levels, altering transportation plans, etc.), thereby leading to more and potentially different problems. A simple way to understand the bullwhip effect is to think of a change in demand as a small wave, that if not proactively communicated, **amplifies** (grows in magnitude and speed) as it reaches further upstream into the overall supply chain.

Vendor managed inventory (VMI) provides a wonderful example of integration and collaboration at an operational level. VMI is an approach where a vendor (supplier) is responsible for deciding when (and how much) to replenish customer inventory (restock), as opposed to the traditional approach where the customer explicitly gives the supplier replenishment directions, often via a purchase order. Let's apply a simple example: Suppose you really love milk (inventory), and you obviously don't want to run out (stockout), nor do you want too much for fear of spoilage (write-off). You could ask your neighbors (supplier) to take responsibility for restocking your refrigerator (warehouse), but how would your neighbors know when to act (replenish), as they obviously live in another house (different company). Well, if your neighbors knew in real time how much milk you presently have (current inventory level) and how much milk you're planning on drinking each of the next few days (planned consumption), then it wouldn't be very difficult at all to understand when a milk run would be needed (no pun intended, but *milk run* is an actual supply chain term describing frequent, small deliveries of inventory). So, what's the key part of this overall example? VMI can only work if the supplier's replenishment plans are integrated with their customer's current inventory level and planned consumption! You now know a simple VMI example that can be applied to an industrial setting.

© rumka_vodki/shutterstock.com

The examples above are meant to highlight the importance of integration and collaboration at the executive level (S&OP), between company functions (ERP), and with external suppliers at tactical (CPFR) and operational (VMI) levels. That's a lot of acronyms—and you now know what they all mean!

Plan

"Planning" is probably the most frequently used term in supply chain management, as in supply chain we plan for so many different things: we plan the industry in which we compete, associated strategy (see the prior chapter), location, and process selection. We also plan capacity, finished goods production, raw materials, packaging, and delivery—and a hundred other things! A key point is that any plan is based on assumptions at a particular point in time. For example, the plan for raw material is dependent upon (or derived from) the finished goods production plan, and the finished goods production plan is dependent upon the customer demand plan. Customer demand in this instance is what is referred to as the ***independent variable***, meaning the variable that, when changed, causes an associated effect on the dependent variable (raw material needs). For these reasons, a common expression in supply chain is "***a plan is the plan until another plan is warranted***." Supply chain is highly dynamic, meaning variables and conditions are constantly changing, hence the need to revisit plans regularly.

© Ivelin Radkov/shutterstock.com

Before we review different planning activities, let's first review different planning horizons, which can be categorized as strategic, operational, and tactical. **Strategic planning** activities generally have timelines beyond one year and are further categorized as being costly and time-consuming to change while also impacting many departments (human resources, accounting, engineering, etc.). An example of a strategic plan is required equipment purchases over the next one to three years in response to <u>anticipated</u> global expansion (see earlier chapter on *Global Supply Chains*). Capacity planning is also an example of strategic planning, as the focus is understanding whether the organization can meet long-term anticipated customer demand.

"A plan is the plan until another plan is warranted"

Oppositely, **operational planning** refers to present time planning decisions—often referred to as the "**here and now**"—and generally includes day-to-day and week-to-week planning activities for the next four to eight weeks. Examples of operational planning include the scheduling of actual production/assembly lines, deciding which inventory items to cycle count (see the upcoming *Inventory Management* chapter), and evaluating whether overtime hours are needed to meet <u>actual</u> customer demand.

Given that strategic planning refers to planning activities beyond a year—and operational planning refers to present-time planning activities—**tactical planning** then refers to planning activities that are in between. As such, tactical planning generally refers to activities beginning two to three months out in the planning horizon, but not beyond a year. An example of tactical planning is developing an inventory plan for the next two quarters or sequencing cost reduction priorities for the latter half of the year. Different companies may have different timelines for the three planning horizons, but the concepts and types of activities are largely consistent. Below is a general timeline of operational, tactical, and strategic planning. Keep in mind, companies may vary in terms of what they call these timeframes and in the timelines themselves. For example, one company may consider operational planning as covering the next eight (8) weeks, while another company may be referring to the next six (6) weeks. In this section we'll discuss strategic planning elements and will defer to later chapters in the book for operational and tactical planning decisions.

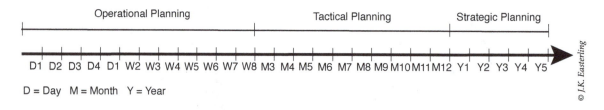

In the earlier *Strategy* chapter, we reviewed the planning activities associated with choosing which industry (*where*) to compete in and an associated strategy (*how*). Choosing the industry and associated strategy are excellent examples of <u>strategic</u> planning decisions, as these decisions fit the criteria of being costly and time-consuming to change while also impacting many departments. Let's now transition to planning the <u>location</u> of our facility(s), which is also a strategic decision.

Choosing the location of a facility—whether it's a manufacturing facility or a warehouse or even a supplier—is a very important decision from a cost perspective as well as an enabler of reliable supply. As such, many large companies now have formal **Supply Chain Network Design and Optimization** (SCNDO) teams that assess alternative plans to enable the lowest overall total cost (Total Cost of Ownership). SCNDO uses modeling software to quantitatively assess various options to derive an overall optimal recommendation. Many colleges and universities that have formal supply chain programs now offer SCNDO courses, which is a hot area within the supply chain profession.

Imagine this scenario: a company is experiencing a drastic increase in sales and needs a new production facility. But where should the new facility be located? There are only a couple thousand possibilities, right!? Think about possible trade-offs: land in rural unpopulated areas may be inexpensive (purchase price only), but there may not be enough prospective employees. Conversely, land in urban areas is typically more expensive, but there may be more accesses to talent. Local and state governments often provide incentives to recruit companies, including reduced property taxes for a period, or assistance with providing training. Access to major highways and interstate systems helps reduce overall transit time and associated logistics costs with replenishing customers. As you can tell, there are many factors that go into planning the location of any type of facility.

Once a location is chosen, **process selection** refers to the acquisition of equipment and setup (layout) of a facility to produce a tangible product (or provide a type of service). Before selecting a process type, two key questions must be answered: what quantity (**volume**) will be needed, and will the process be required to make a narrow or wide range of products/services (**variety**)? Let's now learn about the four major operational process types with an illustrative example of each: job shop, repetitive assembly, batch, and continuous.

© Christina Richards/shutterstock.com

A ***job shop*** is an operational process in which products are made to each customer's <u>unique</u> specification (make-to-order). A common example is a machine shop, where each product is unique, and volume is typically very small—often only one to two pieces. In the coal mining industry, it's rather common for a part to break on an older piece of equipment, leading to considerable downtime and operational inefficiency. These types of replacement parts are not typically available in a "parts store." Rather, a replacement piece must be fabricated, often using the broken piece as a template. Job shops are characterized by high levels of planning complexity, as each customer's order is extremely unique, leading to varying cycle times (time to complete), and are heavily dependent upon the raw materials needed for each customer's unique need. Cost is usually high given the time required to set up equipment to each customer's unique specification, as well as overall complexity with fabricating a new piece, as often "trial and error" is required.

Machine shops further play an essential role in helping innovators bring new products and services from "***conceptualization to commercialization***" by making samples that can be used in demonstrations and trade shows, and by calling upon prospective customers. Interestingly, a hospital is a great service example of a job shop process, as each customer (patient) has a specific and unique need (heart scan, kidney dialysis, maternity ward, etc.).

Repetitive assembly is a process type that gained popularity when the Model T was introduced to the world in 1908. Henry Ford wanted the Model T to be affordable, simple to operate, and durable. The vehicle was one of the first mass production vehicles, allowing Ford to achieve his aim of manufacturing the universal car. The Model T was manufactured on the Ford Motor Company's moving assembly line at Ford's revolutionary Highland Park Plant. Due to the mass production of the vehicle, Ford Motor Company could sell the vehicle for between $260 and $850, as Henry Ford passed production savings on to his customers.[14]

© FlyingDoctor/shutterstock.com

---

[14] Ford Motor Company. (n.d.). The Model T. https://corporate.ford.com/articles/history/the-model-t.html

Repetitive assembly is often used for high-volume/make-to-stock (MTS) items that are standardized, such as automobiles, kitchen appliances, printers, and air conditioners. In make-to-stock environments, products are made to a <u>general</u> customer specification during one period and are used to fulfill customer orders made in a subsequent (future) period. **Decoupling** describes when a product is made in one location but used (consumed) in a different location. Think about the process of shopping for a new stove at your favorite home improvement store. There's not really an option to customize a stove to your unique specifications; rather, one selects a stove based on the options that are available. Repetitive assembly processes are characterized by lower planning complexity given that the product is standardized. With more standardized output, raw materials and packaging uniqueness are minimized as well.

© Joni Hanebutt/shutterstock.com

Batch is a process that has characteristics of both job shops <u>and</u> repetitive assembly processes. Batch processes have more product flexibility than high-volume repetitive assembly processes, yet still make product in lower volumes like job shops. Some supply chain professionals consider batch operations to be a *hybrid* between job shops and repetitive assembly. Batch processes are often characterized by having limited production capacity and capability. A great example of batch operations is a microbrewery. Microbreweries often have frequent job changes—a process where the production line is cleaned and unique raw materials are readied for the next **batch** of beer production, such as pilsner, dark lager, porter, stout, winter or summer ale, etc. Many supply chain professionals think of batch processes as making increments (batch sizes) of one product before transitioning into making another (often related) product. **Economic Production Quantity (EPQ)** is a mathematical approach in batch processes for calculating the size of a production run based on job change costs, inventory holding costs, and annual demand.

© Africa Studio/shutterstock.com

Continuous processes are those that generally operate 24/7/365—usually lacking an *"easy on/off switch"*—meaning once the process begins it's used *continuously* until the end of the asset's useful life, or until the need for a major repair or overhaul. Continuous processes are commonly used to produce oils, gases, iron, chemicals, glass, and some pharmaceutical products. Products made on continuous processes are highly standardized, meaning product uniformity is very high, as is finished goods inventory given the ongoing (continuous) nature of production. An excellent example of continuous production is LCD (liquid crystal display) glass made for smart devices, televisions, laptops, and desktop monitors. LCD glass is made using continuous manufacturing processes that generally run uninterrupted for upwards of 24 months before required repairs/rebuilds.

© Hadrian/shutterstock.com

Below is a table summarizing the four major operational process types. Keep in mind that there's no requirement for a company to only employ one of these processes. A microbrewery, for example, could have a combination of repetitive assembly processes for its high-volume beer (maybe 75 percent of overall volume as an illustration), and then another unit dedicated to making lower volume and more seasonal products (the remaining 25 percent of overall volume). Expected customer <u>volume</u> and <u>variety</u> should be the primary criteria for deciding process type.

	Matrix of Four (4) Major Operational Process Types			
	Job Shop	**Batch**	**Repetitive Assembly**	**Continuous**
Illustrative example	Machine Shop	Microbrewery	Kitchen Appliances	LCD Glass
Degree of Product Specialization	Highly Customized	Moderately Standardized	Standardized	Highly standardized
Distinguishing Characteristic	Traditional make-to-order	Incremental output (batch sizes)	Traditional make-to-stock	No easy 'on/off' switch
Planning & Scheduling Complexity	High	Moderate	Low	Lowest
Finished Goods Inventory	Low	Moderate	High	Very High
Raw Material Uniqueness	Very Unique	Moderate	Low	Lowest
Packaging Complexity	High	Moderate	Low	Lowest

© J.K. Easterling

Continuing with different types of planning, there's also a level of strategic planning that describes the flexibility and autonomy of individual locations within strategic business units (SBUs). Per the illustration below, it's very common for business units to have facilities in multiple countries.

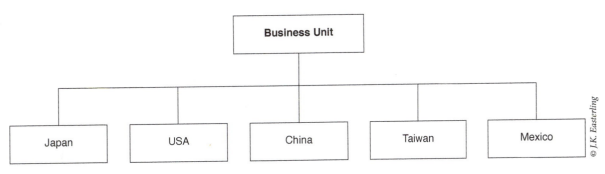

© J.K. Easterling

In **centralized** organizations, major decision making for each location is made at the business unit level (top down), whereas in **decentralized** organizations major decisions are made by management at each location (bottom up). Supply chain decisions include activities such as choosing raw material suppliers, transportation providers, equipment manufacturers, packaging types (e.g., reusable versus disposable), etc. There's also a **hybrid** approach where some (typically more strategic) decisions are made in a centralized fashion, whereas other (typically tactical and operational) decisions are made locally (decentralized). For illustrative purposes, raw material suppliers for all locations might be mandated at the corporate or SBU level, whereas decision making for local transportation or packaging might be relegated to facilities operating in those respective countries.

Planning analysts often perform various forms of **simulation**, which is in essence a form of modeling using different scenarios. For example, a company may run base, optimistic, and pessimistic demand scenarios evaluating the impact of a proposed new pricing strategy on production capacity and inventory levels. Simulation allows an organization to understand potential impacts from various "*what if*" proposals as a proactive means of developing strategies (plans) for success.

As you can now see, *planning* is a highly complicated area within supply chain. Not only do we *plan* many different things (variables), but the need for re-planning occurs regularly. In this section, we focused more on strategic planning for processes that are costly and difficult to change. In the coming chapters, we'll review operational and tactical planning processes for finished goods, raw materials, and packaging.

Source

n this chapter, we'll study the part of the supply chain organization that has primary responsibility for engaging with suppliers. Supply chain professionals who work in the Sourcing pillar are in essence *agents* of their employer (i.e., *principal*), meaning they have the responsibility <u>and</u> authority for negotiating and entering formal contracts on behalf of their employer; this is what's commonly referred to as the *agent-principal relationship*. The agent-principal relationship in supply chain is very similar to professional sports, where an agent represents a given player in contractual negotiations with a professional sports team(s). Great care should be taken to avoid a *conflict of interest*, meaning the agent should not act in a manner that does not wholly benefit the principal. Those who work in sourcing—as in all areas of supply chain management—must be of exceptionally high character in representing the best interests of the employer.

Given that sourcing is *outward facing* (engages heavily with external companies), robust training in ethics and supplier negotiations is required to reduce the likelihood of bribery and other behaviors that could damage the reputation of the employer and/or lead to fines and penalties. There are several things a sourcing professional can do to enable a higher degree of ethics and professionalism, including the following five core concepts:

1. Keep formal (documented) records of all meetings with current and/or prospective suppliers (date, time, attendees, location, topics discussed, outcomes, agreements, etc.). Ideally, two people from each company should be in each meeting to reduce the likelihood of misunderstandings.

2. Pursue <u>external</u> professional certifications and participate in continuing education programs to stay abreast of the latest trends, laws, and ethical considerations across various countries.

3. If a mistake is made (in judgement, computationally, contractually, etc.), document it and take immediate corrective action. The appearance of hiding something is typically worse than the offense itself, as it calls into question one's character.

4. Use extreme caution in having personal relationships with suppliers (dating, attending sporting events, vacations, dinners with spouses, etc.). *"Perception is reality,"* meaning others may judge your relationship as lacking neutrality in the business arrangement or loyalty to the employer (principal).

5. Most companies have regular and required <u>internal</u> Code of Conduct/Ethics training for educating sourcing professionals (including simulated scenarios) in common negotiating practices with suppliers in other countries.

"Perception is reality"

Companies source a wide range of items, including **tangible items** (physical items that can be held and touched, such as raw materials, packaging, and equipment) and **intangible items** (things that generally can't be held or touched, such as janitorial and lawncare services). Before we go much further, let's first distinguish between two terms—buying and sourcing—that are *"related but not the same thing."* **Buying** refers to the acquisition of goods (or services), generally at current market prices (**spot buy**), with payment typically made in cash and at the time of purchase, and without any long-term contract between the buying and selling companies. Essentially there is no commitment between companies; each exchange is simply treated as a singular transaction. Think about when you go to a nice steakhouse or seafood restaurant; typically, the menu lists "market prices," meaning the price of your entree adjusts regularly based on supply and demand, and the price of your meal today might differ from the price of your meal tomorrow. In addition, payment is due at the end of the meal!

Sourcing also refers to the acquisition of goods (or services), but generally a long-term contract exists between the buying and selling companies with predefined pricing, payment terms, and delivery. The supplier may offer additional value-added services, such as providing reimbursement for defective product or assisting with ideas for reducing overall cost (**Early Supplier Involvement/ESI**). Think about a large-scale automobile manufacturer that purchases tires from a supplier. The automobile manufacturer and the tire supplier don't renegotiate the purchase of every single tire or shipment; instead, a contract exists that defines the overall **terms and conditions** (Ts & Cs) between the two firms. A contract may have **tiered pricing**, which means one price exists up to a certain volume (e.g., $40/each up to 250,000 tires), and then a lower price for additional volume (e.g., $38/each from 250,001 to 500,000 tires). Now that we understand some basics, let's dive a bit deeper.

Deciding what an organization does internally (insourcing) versus what it acquires externally (outsourcing) is not solely the job of the buyer, though the buyer does have a major role. A buyer's role is to assist with the <u>quantitative</u> (e.g., performing cost comparisons) and <u>qualitative</u> analysis (e.g., identifying pros and cons) of doing a task or process internally compared to buying externally. Organizations outsource many different things: raw materials, sub-assemblies, transportation, and even some departmental functions such as payroll, cafeteria services, employee recruitment, janitorial services, and customer service call centers. As such, while a buyer should assist with the insourcing/outsourcing analysis, the final decision should be made by senior management after a thorough cost/benefit analysis; this is often referred to as the **make or buy decision**. A general rule of thumb is to outsource those things an external supplier can provide at a lower overall <u>total</u> cost, so long as it does not jeopardize intellectual property or risk the firm's competitive advantage.

Let's learn more about the process of initiating a (prospective) strategic relationship with a supplier(s). Most people—those without specialized supply chain training—simply refer to any formal request (or inquiry) to a supplier as a Request for Quotation/RFQ. But we're <u>not</u> most people, and you'll soon know the differences between three types of requests.

A **Request for Quotation (RFQ)** is a process typically used for requesting a quote for tangible goods with defined specifications, such as raw materials, packaging, or a piece of equipment. Items typically included in RFQs are **direct items**, meaning items that are used directly (physically) in the production of goods or performance of a service.

A **Request for Proposal (RFP)** process is generally used for requesting a prospective supplier(s) to provide a proposal for intangible goods or **indirect** goods or services, meaning products or services that are not used directly in the production of goods. Examples include asking a supplier(s) for a proposal for something routine (e.g., lawncare services) or for something more significant (e.g., new LED lighting to reduce electricity usage).

A **Request for Information (RFI)** is a process often used when the buying company wants <u>preliminary</u> information from a prospective supplier, such as product capability, quality certifications, location of facilities, capacity limitations, delivery capabilities, credit rating, industries served, etc.

For a supplier to provide a legitimate quote, certain pieces of information are needed. Imagine you own a window cleaning business. Suppose a prospective customer calls and asks you for a quote. What information would you need to provide a quote? At minimum, you'd want to know the number of windows, how many windows are accessible without a ladder, how big the windows are, etc. Let's use a simple example of an automobile manufacturer sourcing bolts from an external supplier. Is it enough for the automobile manufacturer to call a prospective supplier and say *"Hey, I'd like to buy some bolts"*? Obviously, the answer is no! What kinds of information would a bolt manufacturer need to provide a legitimate quote? Below are just a few <u>basic</u> considerations for illustrative purposes:

- overall specifications and tolerances, including width and length, thread pattern (pitch), head design (metric or standard), material composition, etc.
- rust inhibitors (e.g., chrome plating, stainless steel, galvanized, etc.)
- torque rating and limitations
- delivery requirements (e.g., daily or weekly)
- quantity needed on a weekly, monthly, or annual basis

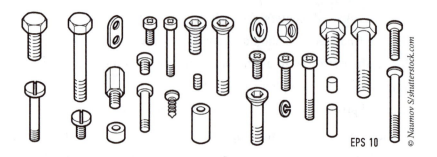

© Naumov S/shutterstock.com

EPS 10

Let's learn the basic steps in requesting quotes (RFQs) from suppliers. This nine-step process provides lots of details on the overall process and introduces many new terms and concepts. In fact, once you understand the process, you might want to consider a career in sourcing—every company needs these professionals!

Step 1: Need Identification - Needs arise in many ways, from the introduction of a totally new product with unique raw materials, to the need for an additional component to solve a quality (existing or potential) problem, to the acquisition of a new style of packaging to reduce long-term total cost of ownership. Needs can arise in a thousand different ways. Supply chain professionals source because a business need exists, either now or in the future.

Step 2: Defined Specifications - To effectively engage and negotiate with suppliers, defined specifications must exist for the item needed, especially if it's a physical good. As per the earlier example with bolts, specifications define clear parameters of what is or isn't acceptable from a supplier. A key point is that supply chain <u>does not</u> define specifications; rather, specifications are typically provided by the engineering organization as an input to the overall RFQ process. Engineering typically provides detailed drawings to aid prospective suppliers in fully understanding specifications, as the surest way to experience undesirable results with a supplier is to provide vague specifications! We'll study the importance of specifications in more depth in the *Make* chapter.

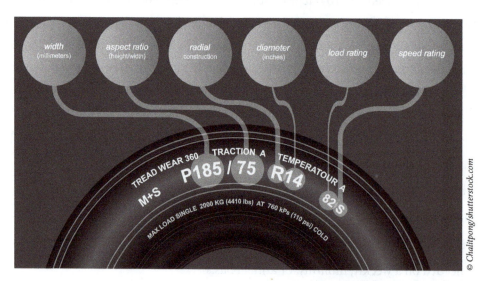

© Chalitpong/shutterstock.com

Step 3: Potential supplier(s) selection - Current suppliers may be chosen to participate in the RFQ process, or possibly new suppliers, or some combination. Companies should do considerable prescreening to identify those prospective suppliers most likely to have interest, capacity, and capability. This step is where the *request for information* process would be highly valuable. Depending on the product (service) and dollar amount, most businesses generally elect to send RFQs to five to seven suppliers. Considerable up-front time should be spent on prequalifying suppliers to ensure a more robust supplier vetting process. Requesting quotes from companies that aren't viable options for whatever reason—credit rating, capacity, capability, etc.—wastes considerable time. Note: before any confidential information is shared, prospective suppliers should sign a formal ***non-disclosure agreement (NDA)*** that establishes legal boundaries preventing them from, for example, selling confidential information to a rival competitor.

Step 4: RFQ (or RFP) Process Initiated - Recall that an RFQ is essentially asking (requesting) a potential supplier(s) to bid on your business need. However, to provide a quote, a supplier needs to have more information about your company's needs and expectations. A supplier would need to know the following variables at minimum to provide a quote:

- annual volume (or perhaps daily, weekly, or monthly)
- required specifications (to ensure quality capability and adherence)
- expected payment terms (when and how will the supplier be paid)
- delivery terms (delivery of goods is not the same as the production or sale of goods)
- whether the buying company will be contributing toward tooling (definition below)
- expectations for reimbursement for defective material

Tooling refers to money provided to the supplier toward the fabrication and/or acquisition of special equipment required to meet the buying company's unique specifications. Contractually documenting which company owns tooling is very important should the need ever arise to change suppliers.

Step 5: Evaluation of RFQs - This step involves collecting and analyzing initial quotes from prospective suppliers. A supplier may genuinely want your business but may not have the capacity (e.g., volume) or capability (e.g., quality) to meet your needs, and in this instance may simply elect to not provide a quote at all. In the spirit of the children's story *Goldilocks and the Three Bears,*[15] quotes typically fall into three categories: "*too low, too high, and just right.*" Let's look at each category.

- **Too low:** A prospective supplier who provides a quote exceeding lower than competitors could be cause for alarm. Perhaps the supplier is desperate for business. Perhaps the supplier misunderstood the required quality. Perhaps the supplier didn't consider shipping (delivery) was required. A quote that is excessively low often indicates some form of misunderstanding or other factors exist.

---

[15] Cauley, L. B. (1981). *Goldilocks and the Three Bears* Putnam Juvenil

- **Too high:** A prospective supplier who provides a quote exceedingly higher than competitors could be cause for alarm as well. Perhaps the supplier doesn't really need the business but is looking to make an excessive profit. Perhaps the supplier doesn't really want the business at the current time, but is providing a quote regardless so your firm may reach out again in the future. Or perhaps the supplier misunderstood some factor(s); for example, they overestimated quality specifications or delivery expectations.

- **Just right:** Sophisticated sourcing organizations, especially those with Global Supply Intelligence (GSI) functions, generally have an idea on market conditions and expected pricing. Focus should be given to those suppliers providing quotes that fall within the expected range of pricing. At the conclusion of the initial RFQ screening, you should have a list of suppliers moving onto the next phase of the sourcing cycle.

© Haso/shutterstock.com

Step 6: Trial Evaluation - This phase of the sourcing cycle involves receiving sample parts and evaluating them in a <u>controlled trial setting</u>. Different industries call this process by different names, but it's generally referred to as **_Failure Mode and Effect Analysis_** (or FMEA). Just like you probably wouldn't buy an expensive new car without test-driving it, FMEA gives the buying company an opportunity to evaluate prospective suppliers' products (or services). Extreme care must be taken to ensure that sample parts are not comingled (mixed) from various suppliers, which would greatly diminish comparison capabilities. Care must also be taken to ensure that finished goods made with trial parts do not make it into the marketplace, as this could create potential for huge liability. Typically, trial parts are destroyed after evaluation, thereby eliminating the risk of potential legal issues from product inadvertently making it into the marketplace. As such, FMEA trials must be conducted in an extremely controlled environment.

Step 7: Supplier(s) Selection - Upon completing the trial evaluation, a supplier should be chosen. Sometimes a single supplier is chosen; however, conditions may warrant choosing a second supplier. **_Dual (or multi-) sourcing_** refers to having two (or more) suppliers for a given product (or service). Dual sourcing helps offset the risk of overdependency on any one supplier. Dual sourcing is often used in the context of having both a foreign supplier as well as a domestic supplier, which helps to provide more supply chain *resiliency*—the ability to respond and/or recover from an unexpected event. Volume does not have to be distributed equally (50/50) in dual-sourcing situations. For example, the foreign supplier might receive 70 percent of the overall business, with the domestic supplier receiving 30 percent of the volume, or some other ratio based on business needs and logic.

Regardless of the number of suppliers, awarding business to a supplier(s) should be done with input from all the relevant departments, such as quality, operations, engineering, and—of course—supply chain. This is consistent with Total Cost of Ownership (TCO) mentality in making major decisions based on multiple inputs and multiple perspectives. A Decision Analysis (DA) is often used for choosing a supplier. *Decision Analysis* is a process in which multiple relevant criteria are evaluated on a supplier-by-supplier base to enable making a holistic (lowest <u>total</u> cost) decision. Below is an example of a decision analysis highlighting three finalists. Note the range of criteria listed on the DA for each supplier; it includes the proposed sales price, delivery cost, reimbursement for defective product, quality certification, and payment term offered. Note that in an RFQ some suppliers may elect to include (*imbed*) certain costs within the sales price (this is common for delivery and tooling in particular). For example, Micah Co. offers a price of $7.26 per piece and delivery is included, whereas the other two prospective suppliers list delivery costs separately.

	RFQ Decision Analysis (DA)		
	RFQ #1 Micah Co.	RFQ #2 Ryleigh Co.	RFQ #3 Allie Co.
Price/per unit:	$7.26	$6.78	$6.98
Delivery included in purchase price? (Y/N)	Y	N	N
if "No," delivery cost per piece:		$0.53	0.31
Reimbursement for Defect?	Yes	No	Yes
ISO Quality Certified Supplier (Y/N)	Yes	No	No
Existing Supplier (Y/N)	Yes	No	Yes
if "No," cost to pre-qualify supplier:		$5,500	
International Supplier? (Y/N)	No	Yes	No
if "Yes," tariff/duty/per piece:		$0.13	
Payment Terms	3/45-N/90	2/10-N/30	2/30-N/45

© J.K. Easterling

Step 8: Contract Finalized - In order for a legally enforced contract to exist, it must be signed by authorized parties from each company. Additionally, companies generally have predefined contractual obligation limitations (sometimes called a *Buying/Sourcing Policy*) that set spending parameters for different levels within the organization. Per below, a Junior Buyer (i.e., entry-level hire right out of college) may have a predefined spending limit of $5,000 per contract (or purchase order). If the contract is $7,500, for example, the contract would need to be signed by a Buyer and reviewed by a Senior Buyer. These types of contractual limitations help ensure that **due diligence**—vetting of supplier, thorough decision analysis, agreement on terms and conditions—is performed <u>before</u> entering a strategic contract that is costly and time-consuming to change.

Contractual Obligation Limitations		
Title	**Spending Limit**	**Reviewer**
Junior Buyer	$5,000	Buyer
Buyer	$10,000	Senior Buyer
Senior Buyer	$25,000	Sourcing Supervisor
Sourcing Supervisor	$50,000	Sourcing Manager
Sourcing Manager	$100,000	Sourcing Director
Sourcing Director	$250,000	VP-Strategic Sourcing
VP-Strategic Sourcing	$500,000	Chief Supply Chain Officer
Chief Supply Chain Officer	$1,000,000	Chief Executive Officer

© J.K. Easterling

Step 9: Ongoing Supplier Management - Effective sourcing professionals, at all levels of the organization and regardless of title, play an active role in managing supplier performance after the contract is signed to ensure that the supplier(s) conforms to overall contractual terms. While leading negotiations with suppliers and developing cost reduction programs are vital, the most important role of a sourcing professional is ensuring **assured supply**, meaning a consistent and uninterrupted supply of material (or services).

An effective sourcing professional also plays an important role in ensuring that suppliers are paid in a timely manner; this process is heavily aided by the implementation of a **three-way match process** that compares the following:

- overall contract with stated terms and conditions
- supplier invoice (document formally requesting payment)
- delivery receipt (document that details what was physically received, e.g., quantity, date/time, condition of delivery, damage, etc.)

A **referral** is essentially a mismatch with contractual terms. As a simple example, the contract may have been written for 500 units at $2.38/each, with 500 physically received (with no defects or other concerns). However, the supplier invoice may have been mistakenly submitted for 5,000 units at $2.38/each (a <u>quantity</u> discrepancy) or 500 units at $2.83/each (a <u>pricing</u> discrepancy). In this instance, the buying company's accounts payable department would not process payment, and therefore, would initiate a referral to the assigned buyer for resolution. In these types of instances, the sourcing professional would simply notify the supplier to resubmit a corrected invoice, subject to agreed-upon payment terms.

Sourcing professionals express payment terms in a unique way. For example, "*2/10, N/30*" means that once a contract exists and delivery is made by a supplier (for each shipment), the buying company can take a two-percent discount if full payment is made within 10 days, otherwise, full (net) payment is required within 30 days. Payment terms have become a heightened focus area, as shortened or extended (longer) payment terms have major cash flow implications to the buying and selling companies. Sourcing has responsibility for negotiating payment terms with suppliers, and conceptually, having a significant payment discount and/or a longer term to pay has major implications for both the buying and selling companies in terms of the **cash conversion cycle** (cash flow).

The sourcing pillar doesn't just have responsibility for choosing a supplier (**supplier selection**), but also has responsibility for ongoing supplier development. **Supplier development** is a process in which the buying company provides timely constructive feedback to enable continuous improvement (kaizen). Most sourcing organizations employ an approach called a **balanced scorecard**, meaning that suppliers are provided feedback on a wide range of areas such as quality (e.g., defect percentage), on-time delivery, billing accuracy, responsiveness to completing corrective actions, early supplier involvement (ESI) with cost reduction initiatives, etc., in order to help gauge overall supplier progress and development. A key point is that the criteria a company uses to evaluate a supplier(s) should be the same criteria that was used to select a supplier. Companies often have **supplier certification programs**, which provide formal recognition and perhaps additional business opportunities for significant period-to-period progress. Sourcing organizations are also further emphasizing environmental sustainability initiatives, with an active environmental sustainability program being part of a supplier certification program.

© Rawpixel.com/shutterstock.com

Sourcing organizations are becoming even more global in terms of identifying world class suppliers and entering formal contracts. With this comes many challenges, namely, possible differences in values and culture. What might be deemed a common sourcing approach in one country may be illegal in another country. As such, many sourcing organizations now have in-house legal counsel that provides real-time advice on contractual terms and considerations. Sourcing organizations continuously search for suppliers across the globe in pursuit of unique capabilities and/or savings opportunities. Most large companies now offer subscription services to databases that provide useful information on conducting business in other countries, such as rules and norms, approaches to decision making, negotiating styles, and organizational structures.

© vichie81/shutterstock.com

Great care must be taken to ensure that a supplier's values align with the buying company's values in order to reduce the potential for reputational risk, embarrassment, and even fines. Many sourcing organizations now employ *Social Responsibility Audits (SRAs)*, an approach of proactively auditing and assessing that a supplier is performing in a manner consistent with the buying organization's values. Frequent international business trips are common for sourcing professionals, as are late-night and early-morning conference calls with suppliers in different time zones. As such, the ability to work efficiently and effectively with suppliers in a global setting is highly desirable.

Operations is the part of the organization responsible for making a physical (tangible) product or providing a service. These are the people who physically work in factories and service organizations. Most products and services require multiple steps that are done in a recurring manner to some degree. For example, a product as seemingly simple as olive oil requires a multi-step operations process consisting of harvesting, washing, crushing, malaxing, centrifugal press, separation, and bottling. Operations is easily one of the most challenging areas of supply chain management. Think about all the work that goes into choosing an industry to compete in (recall the *Strategy* chapter), deciding on the process selection and layout of the facility (recall the *Plan* chapter), hiring and training employees, and a thousand other things, with success (or failure) ultimately dependent upon the group of people who physically make the product or provide the service. Now that's a lot of pressure!

© Macrovector/shutterstock.com

There are in essence two types of products: make-to-stock (MTS) and make-to-order (MTO). *Make-to-stock* products are those typically produced in bulk (large) quantities and to a general customer specification. Shampoo, microwaves, bleach, bicycle seats, wheelbarrows, and candy bars are all examples of make-to-stock items. Conversely, *make-to-order* products are made to each customer's unique specification (need). A custom-tailored suit and new granite countertops (based on a unique kitchen cabinet configuration) are simple examples of make-to-order services (custom alterations) and products (countertops). Automobile repair shops and hospitals are examples of service providers that apply the make-to-order concept, meaning both provide services based on each customer's *unique* specifications (needs).

Before we go deeply into operations, let's first learn about some key decision points—namely *systems design* and *systems operation* decisions. Systems design decisions refer to the initial setup of a process, whereas systems operations refer to the actual day-to-day use of a process. Let's explore each in more detail.

Systems design includes strategic elements such as acquiring equipment, determining long-term capacity needs, picking a site location, and choosing layout. We can use a simple example of building a new factory. The size of the factory (usually expressed in square feet), the location (recall the earlier section on *SCNDO*), process selection (job shop, batch, etc.), and layout (equipment configuration) are all strategic decisions that are time consuming and expensive to change.

Systems operations decisions are more <u>operational</u> and <u>tactical</u>, and include, for example, decisions about hours of operations, which days raw materials are being delivered from specific suppliers, and sequencing customer orders into an overall daily and/or weekly production plan. This chapter focuses more on systems operations issues, meaning the day-to-day and week-to-week challenges faced by operations managers. Operations managers at all levels must be concerned with a whole host of issues simultaneously: changing competitive conditions, new product (service) rollouts, possible supplier raw material shortages, avoiding quality problems, competing in a global economy, ensuring safety of workers, and operating in a sustainable manner (e.g., reducing landfill waste). These are just a few of the ongoing challenges for those who work in operations roles.

The role of quality is essential in operations management. However, quality is somewhat difficult to define in terms of words, and as such, operations professionals use specifications to help ensure <u>conformance</u> and <u>measurability</u>. Imagine working in a continuous manufacturing process (recall the *Plan* chapter) in which molten glass is flowing 24/7/365 (continuously). Further imagine that your customer, a prominent LCD television manufacturer, wants ultra-thin break-resistant glass only 0.7mm thick, which coincidently is thinner than mechanical pencil lead! How can operations ensure they meet the customer's specification? Well, let's first explain what is really meant by a specification, which is one word often used to describe three things that are "*related but not the same thing.*"

- **Variable:** in this case, glass thickness
- **Specification:** in this case, glass 0.7mm thick
- **Tolerance:** in this case, assume the customer communicates +/- .05mm

So, how do we interpret this overall *specification*? For the thickness specification only, the desired thickness is 0.7mm, with a tolerance of +/- 0.05mm, whereas glass as thin as 0.65mm (0.7mm – 0.05mm) and as thick as 0.75mm (0.7mm + 0.05mm) is acceptable. The tolerance defines the *range of acceptability*, which we can plot on a *control chart*—a tool that visually depicts the specification required by the customer and corresponding actual performance. Note that we refer to the minimum acceptable thickness as the *lower control limit (LCL)*, and the maximum acceptable thickness as the *upper control limit (UCL)*. Control charts are a form of *statistical process control (SPC)*, which is used to ensure that a particular process operates efficiently in producing specification-conforming products (and less rework or scrap). Quality Assurance analysts (often called *QA Techs*) monitor the manufacturing process for two critical things: (1) to ensure that product being made meets customer specification; and (2) to highlight when product does not meet customer specifications so <u>proactive</u> measures can be taken.

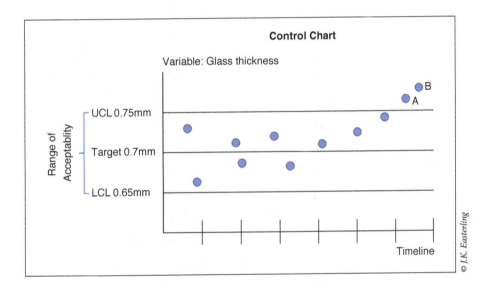

In the control chart above, the blue dots represent actual thickness from individual sheets of glass measured during the manufacturing process. The data shows that nine sheets of glass have thicknesses well within the range of acceptability (within the parameters of the UCL and LCL). You may notice that even with the acceptable sheets that there's some deviation; deviations within the UCL and LCL are referred to as *normal deviations* and are inherent to the manufacturing process. However, data shows that two sheets, referenced as "A" and "B" on the Control Chart, fall outside the range of acceptability; any data points outside this range represents product that will not be acceptable to the customer.

Product made outside the range of acceptability, either above the upper or below the lower, is referred to as **abnormal** (or assignable) **deviations**. The term **assignable** highlights that this deviation was caused by a specific issue, perhaps a machine malfunction or an employee error, whose cause should be <u>identified</u> (assigned) and <u>resolved</u> to reduce future instances. And of course, those two specific sheets of glass (referenced as "A" and "B" on the control chart) should be rejected and not shipped to the customer! By the way, thickness isn't the only variable in the production of LCD glass. Glass weight, overall size (width and length), stress (fracture) point, flatness, and streak (bands of discoloration) are other common specifications. To be approved for shipment, an individual sheet of LCD glass doesn't have to meet the specifications of just <u>one</u> variable, it must meet the specifications of <u>all</u> variables! That's pressure!

The glass example above conveniently highlights that not all products can be reworked. **Rework** is a term that describes <u>additional</u> steps taken to bring a product (or service) into overall specification conformance. Rework is a **non-value-added (NVA)** process, meaning incremental steps and costs are being incurred without the possibility of incremental revenue. Many products cannot be reworked, thereby requiring financial write-off and physical disposal. Many processes that have a **covering** process, for example plating or painting, may **mask** (hide) an underlying quality problem.

Businesses use key performance indicators (KPIs) to guide improvement initiatives to assess current year performance (to prior periods) and to compare themselves to competitors. One of the most used operational metrics is **productivity**, which examines the relationship between inputs and outputs. Productivity is especially important to manufacturing companies, as the **transformation process** of converting inputs (such as raw materials) into saleable outputs (finished goods) is of key importance as a driver of overall profitability. Saleable output represents future revenue, whereas inputs represent cost drivers; together, these variables represent key components of overall firm profitability.

However, evaluating output relative to a singular input is not of great importance. Instead, many firms use **multifactor productivity**, which as the name implies, evaluates output relative to multiple factors (or inputs). Additionally, output is generally measured in number of units produced, whereas inputs are generally measured in dollars. This presents an "apples and oranges" challenge of comparing variables that are expressed in different units of measure (numerator in units; denominator in dollars). This challenge can be easily overcome by converting the numerator output into a modified output variable expressed in dollars.

Efficiency is a highly important concept in supply chain management and refers to how efficient a process is in making saleable product (or providing a service) versus a theoretical baseline. Let's use an example of a manufacturer of a physical good, in this case a microprocessor. A microprocessor manufacturer would know how many units were produced—relative to how many units should have theoretically been produced in some time period—based on underlying assumptions.

Let's use some simple math as this concept is extremely important. Let's assume a microprocessor has a finished goods *cycle time* of 30 seconds, meaning that every minute, two completed microprocessors theoretically should be produced. But what about those *underlying assumptions*? Obviously, the number of days worked per month and the number of hours worked per day (8, 16, 24?) have a great impact on actual and theoretical output. Process selection, facility layout, degree of automation, quality requirements, specifications, etc., would all be important factors as well. Let's assume based on all these factors that the microprocessor manufacturer should have been able to produce 80,640 units last month, whereas they produced 71,840, for an efficiency factor of 89.1 percent (71,840 / 80,640).

There are a few major takeaways here. First, an efficiency factor of 89.1 percent means in essence that the company achieved an inefficiency factor of 10.9 percent, meaning that out of every 100 microprocessors that theoretically should have been produced, 10.9 were not due to various reasons. Over the prior month, that 10.9 percent loss represented the loss of 8800 units (80,640 – 71,840).

The table below highlights the six loss categories. Continuous improvement can only occur when there is reliable information for decision making. By examining the table below, we can easily conclude that supplier issues—defective incoming raw materials and late deliveries—accounted for more than 60 percent of the overall loss. With this information, supply chain professionals in the sourcing area—who have the primary responsibility of managing and engaging suppliers—can take decisive action to drive improvement. This example not only highlights the important role of efficiency, but also the *integration* aspect of how supply chain pillars work together.

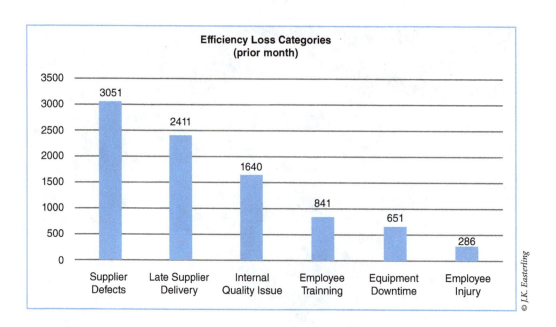

Efficiency Loss Categories (prior month)

© J.K. Easterling

Operations is one of the most challenging areas within supply chain management. Having an "output" (production) plan (what, when, and how many) may seem straightforward, yet ensuring conformance with customer specifications while simultaneously managing multiple "inputs" (labor, equipment, and raw materials) is extremely challenging. Operations managers often have prior experience working in other areas of supply chain, which helps with gaining perspective on how all the supply chain pillars must be integrated in meeting customer requirements.

Deliver

The Deliver pillar provides us an opportunity to learn more about an area of supply chain that is broader and more complicated than most people imagine. It's a common mistake to use the words "logistics" and "transportation" interchangeably, for as we know, those are *related but not the same thing.* Transportation is in fact just one part of logistics, just as logistics is one part of supply chain. Logistics includes activities well beyond the major modes of transportation and includes warehousing and handling; it also includes managing packaging, ensuring product safety, fulfilling customer orders, navigating highly complicated processes for international shipments, and so much more! It's also important to note that in the Deliver pillar, we're primarily focused on *forward logistics*, meaning logistics that move from upstream (suppliers) to downstream (toward customers). The Return pillar focuses primarily on *reverse logistics*, meaning logistics that move in the opposite direction of downstream (customers) toward upstream (suppliers). We'll save reverse logistics for the next chapter.

© DigitalPen/shutterstock.com

Let's start with learning the major modes of transportation. A **mode** refers to the different options available for moving products. The five major modes of transportation are: marine (water), air, pipelines, trucking (motor), and railroad. Interestingly, each mode has its own unique attributes and cost structure. The general trade-offs between these modes are "time" and "cost"—meaning some are faster and more expensive, while others are slower and less expensive. Keep in mind, there is no requirement for an organization to use only one mode of transportation exclusively. In fact, most organizations simultaneously use multiple modes of transportation as warranted in order to meet unique customer needs. Let's review each mode in detail to enhance our overall knowledge!

Marine (water) transportation includes a wide range of ships that navigate oceans, rivers, canals, and other waterways. Ocean cargo ships can now haul upwards of 25,000 containers. Cargo containers are generally measured in terms of **TEUs** (twenty-foot equivalent unit in length), and the most common sizes are 20 and 40 foot in length. Therefore, a 40-foot container would be equivalent to two TEUs. Cargo ships enable large amounts of product to be moved long distances at economical rates. Sometimes an individual container is packed with only one item; conversely, a container may be packed with many different products. Hence, a primary advantage of an ocean container is the flexibility to carry many different types of products, from teddy bears to clothing to patio furniture and everything in between! A major disadvantage of ocean cargo ships is that it may take 18–20 days for one to sail from Hong Kong to Los Angeles, possibly longer if the weather doesn't cooperate.

© Avigator Fortuner/shutterstock.com

There are many different types of ocean cargo ships, including those that specifically move livestock, crude oil, and automobiles. With ocean cargo ships getting bigger and bigger, many ports are now struggling to accommodate the massive lengths. A **port** is a docking place for ships to load/unload their cargo. Imagine trying to "parallel park" a 1300-foot-long cargo ship (equivalent in length to four football fields) loaded with over 25,000 TEUs—now that's skill! Massive cranes are operated by **longshoremen** to load/unload containers. Imagine the weight of a loaded ocean cargo ship. Many ports are now having to dredge their waterways to enable the megaships to navigate. *Dredging* is a process to deepen a water-way by removing soil, mud, rock, and other debris, as illustrated below, to accommodate heavier ships that sit deeper below the water line (*draft*).

Marine transportation includes other types of ships as well, including barges, which typically navigate rivers and canals. Barges are often used for moving bulk cargo such as coal, oil, and various types of grain (corn, wheat, etc.). *Bulk cargo* refers to product that is transported in large quantities without packaging or packing, where the means of transport acts as the container.

Trucking (sometimes called "motor") is the preferred mode of transportation for the movement of goods within 500 miles, primarily due to its great advantage of being able to move product directly from "door to door" (from a pickup point to a destination), as all other modes generally require some type of *unimodal* service (combining two or more modes of transportation). Trucks come in all different types and sizes, from the traditional 18-wheeler to "bread trucks" to trucks that transport coal, gases, and oils ("bulk" items).

© Net Vector/shutterstock.com

Trucking plays a crucial role in local, state, national, and global economies due to its primary advantage of being highly flexible. More and more products are being shipped by trucks, and many countries are reporting shortages of trained truck drivers. Some countries are reducing the required minimum age of truck drivers in anticipation of significant retirements in the coming years. Many trucking companies now offer signing bonuses, pay incentives, and routes that reduce (or limit) the amount of time away from home. Trucking, as with all other modes of transportation, is heavily regulated with size and weight limitations for roads, bridges, and tunnels, etc. Truck drivers are heavily regulated as well in terms of allowable hours on the road on a daily and weekly basis. There are several recent trends in the trucking industry, including the development of *autonomous* (self-driving) trucks, as well as electric and/or hybrid trucks to help with environmental sustainability concerns (as opposed to traditional diesel fuel).

Some companies may elect to outsource transportation to *third party logistic (3PL)* providers. Companies may want to operate their own fleet if the product has ultra-high intellectual property, if the product is highly sensitive to damages, or if they simply choose to have more control over how their products are transported to customers. 3PL providers can be classified into two main categories: *dedicated carriers* that move product for only one customer at a time, or *common carriers* in which a company's product(s) might be comingled with products from other companies (often referred to as *Less-Than-Truckload* [*LTL*]). Shipping product with a common carrier is generally less expensive because the overall shipment cost is being shared by multiple companies. The rate for moving product via a dedicated carrier is more expensive because the entire expense, whether the load is full or not, is fully borne by only one company.

Rail cargo is an effective means of moving product over long routes. Rail has moderate delivery speeds at moderate costs, as compared to air cargo (fast delivery speeds at high costs) and ocean cargo (slow delivery speeds at low costs). Rail also has an advantage of being able to carry many different types of products, including very heavy weights. As with trucking, rail cars come in many different types as well. There are special types of rail cars for moving logs, bulk items (e.g., coal and grains), gases, automobiles—even ocean containers on rail flat cars (appropriately named *Containers on Flatcars* [*COFC*]).

© Denis Dubrovin/shutterstock.com

Military organizations place great emphasis on the use of rail systems in moving extremely heavy product over long distances. Imagine moving 500 large tanks domestically by any other mode! Military organizations greatly value the role of logistics and now offer specialized fields in logistics. Military leaders often refer to logistics as ensuring they have "*beans, band-aids, and bullets*" required to carry out their missions.

Air cargo involves the use of airplanes (and occasionally helicopters) for moving product in an expedited manner, literally the same speed at which people can be transported from one point to another! A major disadvantage is cost, which is often ten times more expensive than container ships. Most companies use air cargo to supplement cheaper modes of transportation (ocean and rail) or in emergency situations. The types of products shipped via air cargo are typically high-dollar items such as jewelry, LCD televisions, cameras, computers, etc. There are obviously weight and size limitations on cargo airplanes. As such, air cargo carriers have **load planners** who determine the overall configuration and loading sequence. Extreme care must be taken to secure air cargo, as any sudden shift in weight can cause a catastrophic air disaster. Extreme caution must also be taken to ensure that certain products are not comingled together on the same flight (or at minimum, safely separated) for fear of combustion or a dangerous chemical reaction (e.g., mixing of ammonia and bleach). Some products, such as lithium batteries and aerosols, must be placed into special sealed containers. Due to these risks, detailed product labeling is extremely important when shipping product by air.

Pipelines are used for transporting products such as oils, gases, fuels, water, etc. Tying to our earlier chapter on manufacturing process types, pipelines are a common delivery system for continuous manufacturing processes (recall the *Make* chapter). Pipelines can be above ground or below ground, and often run for hundreds (sometimes thousands) of miles. Pipelines can also be installed under water. Burying pipelines is gaining in popularity for two primary reasons: to preserve the beauty of natural landscapes (an element of *environmental sustainability*), and as a risk-mitigation technique to reduce the likelihood of tampering and/or sabotage. Pipelines have an advantage in being able to move massive amounts of product literally on a nonstop (continuous) basis. However, a major limitation is only being able to "transport" one unique product (e.g., oil). There are also major upfront costs required to build pipelines, including gaining *right-of-way* access from property owners and the physical installation.

© Maksim Safaniuk/shutterstock.com

Given the massive volume of freight moved across the various modes of transportation, companies often enlist the help of freight forwarders to negotiate capacity and pricing. *Freight forwarders* act as an intermediary between the company that makes the product and the actual transportation provider. A freight forwarder may reserve capacity on a container ship equivalent to 500 TEUs and will then allocate (sell) the 500 TEUs across a wide range of customers. Freight forwarders can also help with the process of generating the necessary documents for efficient clearance through customs.

Some products, such as various types of food and pharmaceuticals, must be transported at cold temperatures to prevent spoilage and decay (referred to as *cold chain*). Refrigerated containers, called *reefers*, are frequently used in marine, motor (trucking), and rail modes. Reefer containers are easily identifiable by built-in cooling systems. Maintenance of reefer containers is very important, for if the cooling system fails, the entire shipment may be ruined.

© Locomotive74/shutterstock.com

Now that we've covered the modes of transportation, let's look at other logistics tasks. Logistics also includes the storage of goods and use of warehouses. Warehousing was once an underutilized area of supply chain, a dimly lit place where large amounts of inventory were held for long periods of time, often with inaccurate inventory records, write-offs, and damaged goods. Those days are long past! Many warehouses today employ various types of robotics for more efficient and accurate processing of receipts (incoming goods) and customer shipments (outbound goods). Today, warehousing is a major driver of operational and financial success via the use of **Warehouse Management Systems (WMS)**, which use a combination of hardware and software systems and tools that are integrated with the company's overall ERP system (see *Supply Chain Integration* chapter).

© studiovin/shutterstock.com

A **cross dock facility** is a type of warehouse where inventory moves in and out very quickly, opposite of the traditional concept of inventory being held for extended periods of time. In cross dock facilities, inventory comes in and is quickly reconfigured into unique outbound loads for purposes of replenishing a certain location or customer. Walmart and other megaretailers commonly use crossdocking processes to optimize replenishing inventory needs of specific stores. In fact, Walmart's logistical proficiency has been widely recognized as a major enabler of the company's overall success.

Warehousing is another one of those *"one size does not fit most"* areas within supply chain. Different companies and different industries have different needs. Some products, such as world-famous Kentucky bourbon, requires extended storage as part of the overall curing process. Bourbon distilleries generally store their barrels in racked warehouses known as **rickhouses**. Rickhouses have barrels stored horizontally on racks, also known as ricks, with room for air circulation around the sides and ends. The buildings are made from a variety of materials such as tin, brick, wood, and concrete, and for the most part lack artificial climate control.

Easterling personal photo, Heaven-Hill Distillery, Bardstown, KY (July 2019)

Warehouses are extremely busy areas, with everything from receiving and inspection of incoming deliveries, to placing items in specific locations for storage (called **slotting**), to prepping outbound customer shipments. Most companies place great emphasis on reducing unsafe acts in warehouse locations, including the implementation of warehouse **safety walks**, a method of proactively identifying potential safety issues that could lead to employee injury and/or product damage.

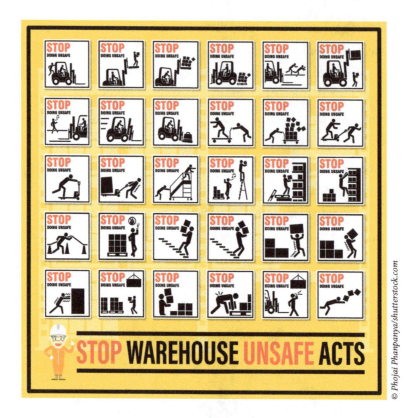

© Phojai Phanpanya/shutterstock.com

The Deliver pillar continues to grow in terms of scope and as an enabler of higher operational efficiency (lower cost, higher profits). Many multinational companies have **corporate control towers** to optimize company-wide decision making in the logistics arena. The term is derived from the control tower concept known in airports across the world, which is a centralized approach for overall coordination. Imagine a company with many different SBUs (see the *Strategy* chapter), with multiple internal SBUs doing business in the same country, for example, Japan. SBUs within a given company don't normally have a lot of engagement, and as such, warehousing and transportation are often unnecessarily duplicated. Control towers enable the overall corporation to identify where SBUs can share global logistics resources to drive higher overall profits.

© Stoyan Yotov/shutterstock.com

Return

As discussed in the last chapter, the Return pillar in essence refers to reverse logistics, meaning logistics that move from customers (downstream) toward suppliers (upstream), which is the opposite of traditional forward logistics. Many supply chain professionals consider both forward and reverse logistics as elements of the Deliver pillar. Regardless, reverse logistics plays a key role in supply chain, hence the reasoning for differentiating between the two.

Reverse logistics may seem like a new concept, but its origins date back decades. Some readers may remember an era when milk was commonly sold in glass bottles and delivered to individual homes, with empty glass milk bottles placed outside the home for pickup and refilling. Some reverse logistics examples are return of goods by customers (either as defects or unwanted goods), return of unsold goods by distribution partners due to contractual terms, reuse of packaging, remanufacturing of goods from returned or defective items, selling of goods to a secondary market in response to returns or overstocking, and recycling and disposal of end-of-life goods.

An excellent example of reverse logistics is returnable (or reusable) packaging, which is a type of multiple-use packaging often used between many B2B companies. Returnable packaging is often made of plastic, metal, wood, etc., and is a popular environmental sustainability initiative as it reduces the amount of disposable packaging deposited into landfills. Returnable packaging isn't just used for sustainability reasons, for while it typically has a higher upfront cost, it tends to have a lower long-term cost due to its reusability. Returnable packaging generally provides more in-transit product safety, thereby leading to fewer damages and customer concerns.

Plastic returnable/reusable packaging (Easterling personal photo)

Another excellent example of reverse logistics is the return of expired ("dead") automobile batteries for recycling. Think of the forward logistics process for a replacement battery: battery is produced, battery is shipped to an auto parts store, battery is purchased and installed. But there's a reverse logistics element as well in that once the battery no longer holds a charge, it's returned to an auto parts store where the customer receives a credit for the "core" return (the physical battery itself). The old battery is then sent to a recycling center, where the lead is separated from the polypropylene (outer plastic shell) and fed into a furnace to be remelted. The lead is then reused to make new batteries. New automobile batteries are typically made with up to 80 percent recycled materials.[16]

© 13_Phunkod/shutterstock.com

A similar reverse logistics example exists with the recycling of smart devices. Most people "upgrade" to a new smartphone every two to three years, even though the old phone is still functional (to some degree). Some people sell or give their old phone to a friend or family member. Many communication

---

[16] Car Battery Recycling (n.d.) Retrieved May 26, 2022, from https://www.autobatteries.com/en-us/installation-and-recycling/battery-recycling

companies now offer an option of allowing customers to trade in their old phone toward the purchase of a new phone. So, what happens to the old phone then? They are often sent to recycling centers and reconditioned (reverse logistics), and then shipped and sold into lesser developed countries (forward logistics), including schools where children can learn all about technology, sports, fashion, and world events. It's pretty amazing to think that the old phone you traded in may be used by two little girls in India who are accessing the internet for the first time! Reverse logistics is all around us if you take time to observe.

© Wirestock Creators/shutterstock.com

Ideally, forward and reverse logistics work in tandem. Returnable packaging is frequently used in the automotive industry between component manufacturers (e.g., suspension products such as shocks and struts) and automobile assembly factories. For example, shock absorbers are typically delivered to automobile manufacturers in returnable containers (forward logistics), and empty containers (from a prior shipment) are loaded right back on the same truck (reverse logistics) for the cycle to repeat, which provides an added benefit of supporting environmental sustainability (upcoming chapter) initiatives and cost minimization.

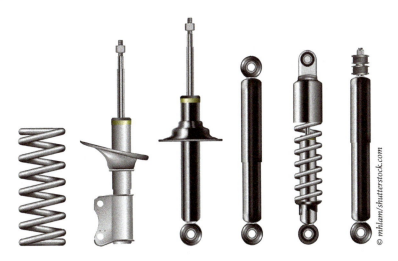

© mhlam/shutterstock.com

We can apply reverse logistics concepts to other supply chain activities as well. Product may be shipped that does not meet a customer's specifications or expectations (see the *Make* chapter) and need to be returned to the manufacturer for rework, sorting, or replacement. A ***return merchandise authorization (RMA)*** allows a customer to return defective or unwanted product, often with the selling company arranging and covering the cost of transportation. In essence, the same thing happens when we as individual consumers buy a product from our favorite online retailer—perhaps a new coat—and then initiate a return because the item doesn't fit, or the color isn't as we expected.

Reverse logistics also helps with environmental sustainability initiatives. Most companies now have recycling initiatives where items such as scrap metal, cardboard, and plastic are collected and shipped back to suppliers for reuse. Reverse logistics also supports the ability to repair, refurbish, recycle, and resell products that are returned, all of which keeps products from ending up in landfills.

© Travel mania/Shutterstock.com

Inventory Management

nventory management is at the very heart of effective supply chain management. A simple definition of inventory is product that currently and physically exists and is available for immediate use and/ or sale. Reflect on the *Introduction to Supply Chain Management* chapter where we discussed supply and demand. Inventory is one of the two components of supply capability. Not only is inventory (of all forms) essential for supply chain management purposes, but it is also a major component of a company's **Balance Sheet**—the financial document that details all assets (and liabilities, too).

Every organization that makes a physical product or provides a service needs an **inventory system** that accounts for activities such as receiving raw materials from suppliers, accounting for work-in-process, verifying scrap or defective product, and managing finished goods. An inventory system must have three elements: an accurate count on current inventory, a bill-of-material (BOM), and a process for projecting future needs (a master production plan).

© Gorodenkoff/shutterstock.com

The first element in an inventory system is an accurate count on all raw materials, work-in-process (WIP), and finished goods inventory. A **cycle count** is a physical verification of actual inventory on an item-by-item basis. Accurate inventory is essential as it's the foundational element of an inventory system. Without accurate inventory as a starting input, the entire inventory system is flawed, leading to what many supply chain professionals refer to as **GIGO** or *"garbage in…garbage out."* Having accurate inventory seems like it should be straightforward, but there are lots of opportunities for discrepancies, hence the need for periodic cycle counts. Most Enterprise Resource Planning (ERP) systems have modules for maintaining and updating inventory records.

The second element in an inventory system is an accurate **bill-of-material (BOM)**, which is a listing of all the raw materials, sub-assemblies, and packaging and their respective usage that goes into making one unit of a particular finished good. A BOM is in essence a parts list, or a **recipe** for making one finished good. Think about making a cake. A cake doesn't magically appear; rather, individual ingredients are used such as eggs, butter, flour, sugar, and other defined ingredients, which are referred to as **raw materials**.

© Kingmaya Studio/shutterstock.com

Once we mix all the raw materials together and pour the batter into a cake pan and place it in an oven, it's now referred to as **work-in-process**. WIP refers to something that is in the **transformative** state of being converted from one thing (individual raw materials) into something else (the cake itself). And of course, once the cake comes out of the oven, cools, and is beautifully decorated, supply chain professionals would say it is now a **finished good**, meaning something that is ready and available to be sold to a customer (*ATS*). The image below captures all three primary types of inventories, from raw materials to work-in-process, to the finished good!

© irina2511/shutterstock.com

The third element of an inventory system is a finished goods production plan, often referred to as **master production plan (MPP)**. A master production plan is a forward-looking schedule detailing how many units are planned to be made in each period (today, tomorrow, this week, next month, etc.). As we learned in earlier chapters, a demand plan is dependent upon a sales plan, and sales plans are a combination of firm customer commitments and future projections (forecasts).

Now that we have a good understanding of inventory <u>systems</u>, we need to think more about inventory <u>cycles</u>. A cycle is something that follows a specific process and repeats. Think about the cake example again in terms of using eggs (raw material) as part of the transformative process of making a cake. In other words, as we make a cake (finished good), we consume eggs (raw material), and therefore need ongoing replenishment of more eggs! It's a cycle!

So how does the replenishment process work? Thankfully, there's a process called **Material Requirement Planning (MRP)** that is used specifically for managing inventory cycles. MRP uses the three primary components of an inventory management system—inventory records, a bill-of-material, and a master production plan—to derive a plan for raw materials, sub-assemblies, packaging, etc.

There are two iterative processes within MRP, one for calculating **gross material requirements**, and one for calculating **net material requirements**. Recall from your payday that *gross pay* means before any deductions (such as taxes, health care, retirement, etc.), whereas *net pay* means after deductions. MRP works much the same way. Let's use our cake example to learn more. In the illustration below, the master production plan shows the number of planned cakes for a four-week period, based on a sales plan that might include weddings, conventions, community events, school programs, etc. Using a simple example that all cakes are the same size and that each cake takes exactly two eggs, we can easily calculate our gross material requirement. Keep in mind the difference between gross and net, though. Gross material planning doesn't take into consideration how many eggs are already on hand, how many are on order, the likelihood of breaking some eggs in the process, etc. This is where net material requirements come into the equation by factoring in other relevant variables.

	Week 1	Week 2	Week 3	Week 4
Master Production Plan (# cakes):	46	48	52	60
Eggs needed/per cake:	2	2	2	2
Gross Material Requirement (number of eggs needed):	92	96	104	120
	↓	↓	↓	↓
Planned consumption:	-92	-96	-104	-120
Expected yield loss:	-5	-5	-5	-5
On order from supplier:	72	144		
Eggs on hand (starting inventory):	68			
Projected inventory level:	43	86	-23 A	-148 B

Net Material Requirement (bracket grouping: Planned consumption, Expected yield loss, On order from supplier, Eggs on hand (starting inventory), Projected inventory level)

+68
-92
-5
+72
=43

© J.K. Easterling

The example above quantitatively highlights the overall process using basic calculations. The -5 eggs each week is meant to represent projected *yield loss,* meaning not all raw materials are efficiently used in the production of finished goods. In this instance, history might indicate five eggs each week are dropped, defective, or unusable in some form or fashion. With this logic, five <u>additional</u> eggs per week are needed to account for yield loss. And lastly, we must account for what is on order (or due to be delivered) for each respective week. The chart shows that 72 eggs are on order in Week 1 and 144 eggs are on order in Week 2. The projected negative inventory levels (represented by the red "A" and "B") means that unless more eggs are ordered and delivered (inventory replenished), the bakery will be short by those quantities of eggs, and therefore won't be able to complete the master production plan or fully satisfy customer orders. In other words, net material requirement planning highlights when "*action*" (supplier replenishment) is needed and by "*how much*" (quantity).

Notice the word "*projected*" inventory level at the end of each week. We use the word "*projected*" inventory for two primary reasons: (1) these are future-looking weeks that haven't happened yet, and (2) the projections are based on various assumptions. Think about the projected 43 eggs at the end of Week 1. What variables could change that would cause that number to be different (either bigger or smaller)? There are four obvious answers:

1. The beginning inventory of eggs was incorrect, hence the need for periodic cycle counts to physically verify inventory levels.

2. The bakery made more (or fewer) cakes than originally planned based on actual customer demand.

3. Yield loss (i.e., dropped eggs) was higher (or lower) than originally expected.

4. The egg supplier was late and maybe didn't deliver the full 72 expected in Week 1. Or, the supplier was early and delivered some of Week 2's orders in Week 1.

The example above of a bakery simply and perfectly highlights the **dynamic** nature of material requirement planning, that being, variables are constantly changing, and therefore need replanning on a regular basis. If you followed the basic mathematical logic and deductive reasoning, you might want to consider becoming an Inventory Analyst—every company needs them! The overall inventory management process is essentially the same for all products from smartphones to computer printers to automobiles.

Effective inventory management processes are critical for supply chain management at all levels—raw materials, sub-assemblies, packaging, finished goods, etc. Inventory is a key component of a company's overall customer service plan. Most companies have a formal **inventory policy** that determines, for example, the minimum and maximum (often referred to as "*min/max*") levels of inventory on an item-by-item basis. Inventory is often referred to as **tied-up capital**, meaning money that is currently being held, for example in raw materials, that will ultimately be consumed in the production and sale of finished goods. The question isn't whether to have inventory. Rather, the questions are "*how much?*" and "*how do we minimize?*"—These are the perfect questions to segue to our next chapter introducing lean concepts.

© Blue Planet Studio/Shutterstock.com

Lean

In the *Make* chapter, we learned about productivity, which examines the relationship between inputs and outputs, and we discussed the apparent advantages of minimizing the inputs (e.g., lower investment in labor, raw materials, equipment, etc.) while maximizing the output (e.g., more saleable finished goods). *Lean* goes a step further by identifying a set of tools that can be used to reduce waste in any type of environment. Lean, however, isn't any singular tool or concept, but a host of tools and concepts that are available for a wide range of challenges and issues. Consider the photo of a tool belt below. Is a screwdriver used to cut metal wiring? No! Is a measuring tape used to hammer a nail? No! Is a wrench used to measure the length of a piece of wood? No! Each tool has a specific function for accomplishing a specific task. In this chapter, we'll learn about some specific lean tools that organizations use to help reduce waste.

© AlexeiLogvinovich/shutterstock.com

At minimum there are three requirements for operating in a lean manner: empowered employees, a reduction of wastes, and a relentless focus on continuous improvement (kaizen). The first requirement is empowering employees by giving them the **authority** to make changes to accomplish specific objectives. Too often management holds people **responsible** for accomplishing a certain mission (or task) but doesn't **empower** them to act. Think about our earlier conversation around operations, those people in the organization directly responsible for physically making the product or performing the service. We can use our earlier example of an automotive assembly line. The people working on assembly lines are the ones most likely to recognize safety issues, identify potential quality problems, and develop ideas for increasing output. Empowerment means giving those people directly responsible for a mission or task the *responsibility* and *authority* to implement ideas for continuous improvement (kaizen).

The second requirement refers to reducing **wastes**, which are typically categorized into seven areas. Let's go through these wastes with a simple example of each for illustrative purposes.

1. **Defects:** Making product that doesn't meet customer specifications (product the customer is unwilling/unable to accept).

2. **Overproduction:** When product is produced faster or in greater quantities than customers want, the risk of write-offs and/or obsolescence increases; may need additional warehouse space (a ***non-value-added*** [NVA] expense).

3. **Waiting:** Bottlenecks cause an unbalanced flow of product/services as well, leading to inconsistent processing times (waiting and delays).

4. **Over (extra) processing:** Rework of a product is an example of an NVA process in that extra processing is required to correct a prior mistake with <u>no</u> offsetting increase in a higher sales price.

5. **Inventory:** Excessive levels of raw material, WIP, or finished goods tie up capital (cash) that could be used for more constructive purposes.

6. **Motion:** Process steps that don't add value (e.g., poor facility layout), thereby leading to unnecessary movements of people (ergonomic issues); for example, walking, bending, or reaching repetitively.

7. **Transportation:** Movement of materials that doesn't add value; for example, moving product to off-site warehouses due to unnecessarily high levels of inventory.

OVER PRODUCTION
TRANSPORTATION
MOTION
WAITING
OVER PROCESSING
INVENTORY
DEFECTS

© Olivier Le Moal/shutterstock.com

The third requirement for operating in a lean manner is a relentless focus on continuous improvement. Continuous improvement can't be a *feeling* (subjective). Rather, it must be measurable and defendable (objective). An organization can only confirm continuous improvement with data. As discussed earlier in the book, we shouldn't conclude success (or failure) by looking at any one variable (e.g., quality defects) without associating it with its related variable (e.g., output). For example, only when we look at defects and output in unison can we accurately conclude progress.

To truly operate in a lean manner, **underlying problems** must be resolved. Below is a very well-known illustration amongst supply chain professionals. Let's review each panel (A, B, C) in detail.

A   B   C

Used with permission of McGraw Hill LLC, from Operations Management, 14e, *William J. Stevenson, © 2021; permission conveyed through Copyright Clearance Center, Inc.[17]*

Panel A highlights that the management team (people in the boat) of a specific company (the boat) often carry higher levels of inventory (waterline) than they otherwise should be due to underlying problems (rocks/boulders). Inventory is an asset that ties up capital (cash), which inhibits a company from doing other value-added tasks—such as providing employees additional training, expanding product/service offerings, or purchasing additional equipment for optimizing quality.

Panel B illustrates that once the inventory level is lowered (waterline), underlying problems (rocks/boulders) become much more visible. Underlying problems—meaning inappropriate reasons for carrying inventory—include things such as unreliable suppliers, poorly maintained equipment, untrained employees, poor forecast accuracy, inconsistent quality, transportation unreliability, ignoring seasonality, lack of market understanding, overly complex supply chain network design, raw material constraints, poor purchasing decisions, etc. To reuse a word from earlier in the book, high inventory levels in essence *mask* (hide) underlying problems. Think about it this way: why should a company carry higher levels of inventory because of an unreliable supplier? It shouldn't—at least not for long! Instead of masking the problem, the focus should be on working with the supplier on a development program (see the earlier chapter on *Source*). A great rule of thumb in supply chain is ***"Never let another company's problems—either upstream or downstream—become your company's problems indefinitely."***

[17] Image courtesy of McGraw-Hill Publishing. *Operations Management*, William J. Stevenson, 14th Edition 2021 McGraw-Hill/Irwin. Pg. 619. ISBN13: 9781260238891

Panel C highlights that once underlying problems (rocks/boulders) have been reduced (it's virtually impossible to eliminate wastes completely), the company (boat) can now efficiently operate with lower levels of inventory (waterline), thereby freeing up capital to pursue other initiatives (like giving bonuses to high-performing supply chain professionals!).

Lean concepts are all around us if we just take time to observe. The paint industry has been completely transformed over the past few years from push to pull. **Push systems** are those that build product (inventory) in anticipation of an eventual customer order. For decades, decisions on paint colors were made far removed from actual customers, leading to massive levels of colored paints being pushed into hardware stores across the nation. Given the inherent conflict between supply and demand, paint was often heavily discounted to incentive customers to purchase slow-moving colors. The paint industry transitioned to a pull system—a lean concept— where customized paint decisions are made at the point of customer purchase. This type of pull system is called **postponement**, and what is being "postponed" is **customization**—waiting until the very last minute to tint the paint based on actual customer demand (as close to the purchase point as possible).

© RossHelen/shutterstock.com

To operate in a lean manner is a <u>conscientious</u> decision, one that is deliberately (intentionally) made. Lean doesn't just happen. Instead, underlying problems that inherently lead to carrying higher levels of inventory must be resolved. A relentless focus on internal continuous improvement is required, as well as with external upstream and downstream partners. Careful decisions should be made in the selection of suppliers, which ties to earlier concepts covered in the *Source* chapter on choosing suppliers based on a holistic approach (Total Cost of Ownership), as opposed to choosing a supplier based on purchase price alone.

Chapter 14

Environmental Sustainability

A growing movement over the past few years has been toward more corporate concern for *environmental sustainability*, which focuses on conserving and protecting ecosystems for current and future generations. Supply chain organizations play a key role in this area through the actions and behaviors taken internally, as well as through the actions with upstream and downstream partners. In this chapter, we'll discuss examples of supply chain initiatives that enable environmental sustainability. An extremely important point is that in many instances, sustainability initiatives help improve the **bottom line** (higher profits). For many years, companies perceived sustainability initiatives as *"right for the planet"* but at a higher cost for the company. Many companies are now finding that these initiatives help improve overall financial performance. Simply put, it doesn't have to be *profits* <u>or</u> *planet*—it can be both!

© VectorMine/shutterstock.com

A recent trend in planning for new facilities, whether manufacturing locations or warehouses, is proactively including sustainability initiatives in the design and construction from the onset, as opposed to retrofitting (reactive) it. As is usually the case, preplanning (forward planning) yields opportunities to design initiatives into the process, as opposed to an "add-on." Many manufacturing companies, for example, use substantial amounts of water, either in the production process itself or in the upkeep and maintenance of the facility. Depending on the robustness of local utility infrastructure, water supply can be an issue. As such, many companies are now constructing facilities with pitched roofs that direct rainwater to retention basins for use in lawn care, in certain types of cleaning, and in some parts of the actual operations process. Additionally, many companies are now adding natural habitats for wildlife adjacent to facilities, and even vegetable and fruit gardens for employees. More companies are moving toward rooftop gardens, which further helps with regulating heating and cooling.

© D-Krab/shutterstock.com

One of America's oldest beer manufacturers, Anheuser-Busch (founded in 1852), is a leader in environmental sustainability initiatives. With over 120 facilities throughout the United States, in 2018 the company set aggressive goals for 2025 in four strategic areas: sustainable agriculture, water stewardship, renewable electricity and carbon reduction, and circular packaging. Anheuser-Busch's sustainability initiatives follow the SMART approach (see the *Strategy* chapter) with specific, measurable, attainable, relevant, and time-bound objectives, two of which are listed below for illustrative purposes. Note that the returnable packaging objective ties directly to what was shared earlier in the book (see the *Return* chapter).

- **Renewable Energy and Carbon Reduction:** 100% of our purchased electricity will come from renewable sources and CO_2 [carbon dioxide] emissions across our value chain will be reduced by 25% by 2025.

- **Circular Packaging:** 100% of our packaging will be made from majority recycled content or will be returnable by 2025.

Note that Anheuser-Busch has the equivalent of an environmental sustainability "mission statement" (below), and that it specifically references downstream (consumers) and upstream (suppliers) partners, highlighting the end-to-end supply chain concept, which you learned about in the introductory chapter. More companies are sharing environmental sustainability initiatives on their respective websites, which highlights the significance of this growing area.

Anheuser-Busch continues to actively engage upstream (suppliers) and downstream (customers) partners to reduce its global footprint. "A healthy environment and thriving local communities" are major objectives for their worldwide production facilities, and they "aim to make a big impact with a small footprint" through their collective efforts across their internal and external supply chain network.[18]

© DenisMArt/shutterstock.com

The Hershey Company—one of the world's largest chocolate manufacturers—was founded in 1894 in Pennsylvania and has a long history of environmental sustainability initiatives. Hershey's sustainability initiatives include programs to protect the environment, including investing in renewable energy, advancing sustainable packaging solutions, protecting water sources, and ending deforestation. Hershey also uses the SMART approach to objectives setting. Note that just as with Anheuser-Busch, Hershey specifically references moving toward more recyclable, reusable, returnable packaging.

- **Advancing Sustainable Packaging Solutions:** In 2015, we committed to reducing packaging weight by 25 million pounds by 2025. We're proud to say we've achieved this goal and have set a new goal of reducing an additional 25 million pounds by 2030. We're also aiming to make 100 percent of our plastic packaging recyclable, reusable or compostable by 2030.[19]

[18] Anheuser-Busch (n.d.). *Environmental Sustainability: A More Sustainable Future*. https://www.anheuser-busch.com/community/environment/

[19] The Hershey Company. Protecting Our Planet's Resources—Safeguarding Our Future. https://www.thehersheycompany.com/en_us/home/sustainability/sustainability-focus-areas/environment.html

**"There's not a person alive who should not plant a tree.
Not for the shade that you'll enjoy, but for those coming after."**

–Milton Hershey (founder)

© Alizada Studios/shutterstock.com

As mentioned earlier, sustainability initiatives can lead to improved financial performance. The production of glass essentially involves earthen materials (mainly sand) super-heated into a molten state and then formed into specific shapes and sizes. A glass bottle may take over 4,000 years to naturally decompose. As such, glass that does not meet customer specification leads to major disposal issues. Glass that is crushed for disposal purposes is called *cullet*. Some glass manufacturers have found an alternative to landfills, as finely crushed cullet can be mixed with asphalt for paving roads and highways, in essence reducing costs while improving environmental sustainability.

"It doesn't have to be profits <u>or</u> planet—it can be both!"

As part of the sourcing cycle, many companies now prioritize suppliers who also have environmental initiatives. The presence of supplier sustainability programs is often included in the request for quotation (RFQ) process and the overall decision analysis. Just as supply chain collaboration should extend end-to-end (upstream and downstream), so too should sustainability initiatives. In fact, the benchmarking of sustainability programs and site visits could and should be a topic of discussion in Collaborative Planning, Forecasting, and Replenishment (CPRF) programs (see the *Supply Chain Integration* chapter).

Analytics

Supply chain management is a heavily data-intensive profession. While experience and managerial judgment is highly valuable, business decisions are primarily based on data, and more specifically, information extracted from data. Most people mistakenly use the terms *data* and *information* interchangeably. You guessed it—these things are "*related but not the same thing.*"

Analytics is a lot like the children's story (and subsequent movie), *Charlie and the Chocolate Factory,*[20] where children strive for the "*golden ticket*" that will bring transformational change to their lives. Companies have thousands of data records on shipments, defects, output, purchase orders, yield loss, pricing, inventory, and customer service—but only a select few (percentage-wise) records in each category have the power to provide transformational change in terms of lower total cost, higher customer service, and improved profitability and competitiveness. That's what analytics does—it finds the proverbial "*golden ticket.*"

© Flame of life/Shutterstock.com

---

[20] Dahl, R. (2016). *Charlie and the Chocolate Factory*. Puffin Modern Classics.

Imagine a large multinational company with thousands of purchase orders each year across multiple locations, from raw materials to paper towels to consulting services and everything in between. The records comprising all those orders—purchase price, supplier, date, location, etc.—are what we refer to as **data**. But it's what we do with the raw data that matters. Sorting, categorizing, analyzing, and interpreting data leads to useful **information** for decision making. Supply chain professionals at all levels use analytical tools and techniques to gauge historical and current performance compared to objectives, but more so, as inputs to forward-looking decisions and continuous improvement (kaizen).

As discussed earlier, in business it's essential never to make major decisions by looking at only one variable, as one variable may not provide the full context and may lead to a poor decision. Let's analyze three variables: internal defects (units), units produced, and defect percentage. If we're only looking at one variable—in this case, the number of internal defects (in units)—the chart below would be of great concern, for we see a very clear upward trend over the last 12 months, which we know is not a good thing.

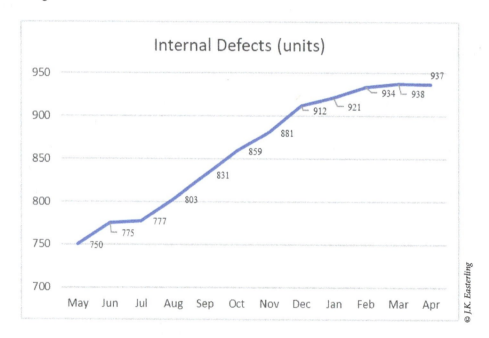

However, simply looking at the number of internal defects without relating it to the number of units produced is naïve, and in fact, downright misleading. Let's examine why. Analyze the data in the table below, and what do you notice? Yes, the number of internal defects is increasing in terms of a raw number, but so too are the number of units being produced. Performing basic analytics shows us that the overall defect <u>percentage</u> has consistently decreased, which means the number of units produced increased at a faster rate than the number of internal defects, which is a very good thing! This example perfectly highlights the importance of examining related variables and never making an important decision by examining any one variable alone.

	May	Jun	Jul	Aug	Sep	Oct	Nov	Dec	Jan	Feb	Mar	Apr
Internal Defects (units)	750	775	777	803	831	859	881	912	921	934	938	937
Production Output (units)	23,500	24,675	25,909	27,204	28,564	29,993	31,492	33,067	34,720	36,456	38,279	40,193
Defect %	3.19%	3.14%	3.00%	2.95%	2.91%	2.86%	2.80%	2.76%	2.65%	2.56%	2.45%	2.33%

© J.K. Easterling

Most supply chain organizations seek to have a **balanced scorecard**, which means performance is assessed across a wide range of key variables rather than only a few. Supply chain variables that are often analyzed include customer demand, inventory, forecast accuracy, capacity (utilization and efficiency), output, defects (both internally and externally), customer returns, and financial performance. There is not a *"one size fits most"* for every company, but rather supply chain organizations should seek to have a balanced scorecard approach that supports and drives specific company goals (reflect on the *strategic fit* concept). Supply chain organizations should use caution, however, not to develop **analysis paralysis**— which means having such an obsession with analytics that it inhibits decision making (this is sometimes referred to as *"not being able to see the forest for the trees"*).

Regardless of business discipline (e.g., accounting, human resources, sales, etc.)—but especially in supply chain management—the ability to establish priorities and effective time-management skills are essential. Supply chain professionals simply have no shortage of things to work on, and as such the ability to prioritize and work on the most important things is vital. Supply chain is a functional area with a heavy emphasis on *"working smarter."* A highly beneficial way to identify areas of highest impact is through a **Pareto analysis**, which takes a large set of raw data and converts it into useful information for decision making.

Below is a Pareto chart highlighting a hypothetical example of the number of instances of employees quitting within two years of hire. We can see that there are six categories (reasons) why employees quit within two years of hire, but by converting the raw data into useful information for decision making, we can see that—by far—the major reason employees quit is due to unhappiness with their direct supervisor. What else can we conclude? Well, initially we can conclude that all the other instances are roughly equal in terms of three to five instances per category. What can we further conclude? We certainly need to prioritize understanding why so many employees quit over unhappiness with their direct supervisor and take some actions, such as possibly providing additional training for all supervisors.

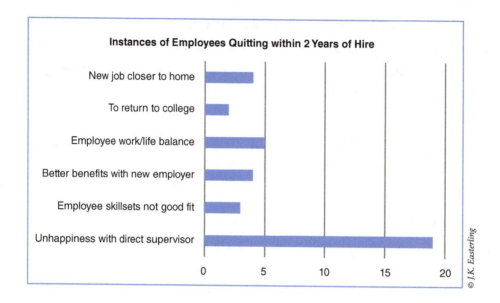

Instances of Employees Quitting within 2 Years of Hire

© J.K. Easterling

ABC analysis provides an opportunity to highlight the power of analytics. **ABC analysis** is a form of Pareto analysis in which large data sets are categorized (sorted) in terms of predefined criteria—annual usage, current (actual) inventory, or dollars (or a combination of all three). In keeping with the approach to this whole book, let's use a simple example to illustrate.

The data table below highlights annual usage for 64 parts (let's assume raw materials, each with a different function) used throughout the year by a hypothetical company. The table shows the ItemID (i.e., part number), supplier name, annual usage, and purchase price per piece. Suppose that at this hypothetical company, their leadership team defines A items as the top 50 percent of annual spend, with B items the next 30 percent, and C items as the lowest 20 percent of annual spend.

© robuart/shutterstock.com

Item ID	Supplier	Annual Usage (pcs.)	Purchase Price/pc.	Annual Spend ($)	$ Cumulative	% of Total (Cumulative)	Class
				Completed ABC Table Highlighting Spending Pareto Analysis			
Item 24	Wilson	269,023	$1.32	$355,110	$355,110	10%	A
Item 12	Costentino	110,879	$3.01	$333,746	$688,856	19%	A
Item 8	Griffin	148,008	$2.13	$315,257	$1,004,113	28%	A
Item 56	ARobinson	250,231	$1.24	$310,286	$1,314,400	37%	A
Item 60	Howard	99,231	$2.65	$262,962	$1,577,362	44%	A
Item 46	Venable	75,892	$2.69	$204,149	$1,781,511	50%	A
Item 58	Peyton	199,121	$0.66	$131,420	$1,912,931	54%	B
Item 59	Rabbe	90,356	$1.40	$126,498	$2,039,430	57%	B
Item 53	Logue	253,502	$0.49	$124,216	$2,163,646	61%	B
Item 5	CRobinson	59,494	$1.85	$110,064	$2,273,709	64%	B
Item 4	CRoberts	68,787	$1.60	$110,059	$2,383,769	67%	B
Item 57	Sedlatschek	69,000	$1.30	$89,700	$2,473,469	70%	B
Item 54	Bronaugh	69,000	$1.29	$89,010	$2,562,479	72%	B
Item 2	Litkenhus	46,920	$1.69	$79,295	$2,641,773	74%	B
Item 47	Hill	35,324	$2.12	$74,887	$2,716,660	76%	B
Item 22	DStanley	54,111	$1.12	$60,604	$2,777,265	78%	B
Item 33	Gadd	23,258	$2.60	$60,471	$2,837,735	80%	B
Item 6	Benton	23,258	$2.56	$59,540	$2,897,276	82%	C
Item 18	Dixon	18,000	$2.91	$52,380	$2,949,656	83%	C
Item 45	Gamba	73,723	$0.54	$39,810	$2,989,466	84%	C
Item 19	Middleton	17,599	$2.12	$37,310	$3,026,776	85%	C
Item 40	Jernigan	17,525	$2.12	$37,153	$3,063,929	86%	C
Item 15	Hershberger	14,870	$1.88	$27,956	$3,091,885	87%	C
Item 36	JRoberts	43,005	$0.65	$27,953	$3,119,838	88%	C
Item 9	Reeves	27,001	$0.99	$26,731	$3,146,569	89%	C
Item 49	Hostettler	17,541	$1.49	$26,136	$3,172,705	89%	C
Item 34	Slater	14,002	$1.69	$23,663	$3,196,368	90%	C
Item 23	Ferguson	12,500	$1.62	$20,250	$3,216,618	91%	C
Item 55	Barger	8,599	$2.16	$18,574	$3,235,192	91%	C
Item 44	Jones	3,573	$5.12	$18,294	$3,253,486	92%	C
Item 16	Fisher	8,800	$1.85	$16,280	$3,269,766	92%	C
Item 3	Coleman	19,000	$0.81	$15,390	$3,285,156	93%	C
Item 51	Price	12,332	$1.20	$14,798	$3,299,954	93%	C
Item 32	Merilatt	5,900	$2.39	$14,101	$3,314,055	93%	C
Item 13	Scott	9,023	$1.56	$14,076	$3,328,131	94%	C
Item 25	Merrihew	8,888	$1.50	$13,332	$3,341,463	94%	C
Item 61	Gousha	8,400	$1.58	$13,272	$3,354,735	94%	C
Item 21	Turner	7,581	$1.62	$12,281	$3,367,017	95%	C
Item 35	Duerr	22,258	$0.55	$12,242	$3,379,258	95%	C
Item 17	Leuthner	6,585	$1.80	$11,853	$3,391,111	95%	C
Item 27	West	7,611	$1.55	$11,797	$3,402,909	96%	C
Item 26	Cramer	6,878	$1.54	$10,592	$3,413,501	96%	C
Item 38	Saylor	53,851	$0.19	$10,232	$3,423,732	96%	C
Item 30	Schoulthies	4,155	$2.40	$9,972	$3,433,704	97%	C
Item 43	Finley	2,250	$4.12	$9,270	$3,442,974	97%	C
Item 1	Perri	7,888	$1.15	$9,071	$3,452,046	97%	C
Item 52	Suggs	3,530	$2.49	$8,790	$3,460,835	97%	C
Item 28	Rose	8,555	$0.98	$8,384	$3,469,219	98%	C
Item 29	Spade	7,487	$1.09	$8,161	$3,477,380	98%	C
Item 39	Thompson	6,526	$1.25	$8,158	$3,485,537	98%	C
Item 11	Schyns	5,878	$1.25	$7,348	$3,492,885	98%	C
Item 31	Combs	5,611	$1.20	$6,733	$3,499,618	99%	C
Item 62	Perry	5,901	$1.07	$6,314	$3,505,932	99%	C
Item 10	Brady	6,555	$0.95	$6,227	$3,512,160	99%	C
Item 14	Hollen	5,487	$1.09	$5,981	$3,518,140	99%	C
Item 48	Ward	10,414	$0.55	$5,728	$3,523,868	99%	C
Item 50	Burlcs	40,481	$0.14	$5,667	$3,529,535	99%	C
Item 20	SStanley	29,130	$0.19	$5,535	$3,535,070	100%	C
Item 42	Closterman	2,311	$2.35	$5,431	$3,540,501	100%	C
Item 63	Yates	3,251	$1.10	$3,576	$3,544,077	100%	C
Item 64	Ruholt	1,598	$2.15	$3,436	$3,547,513	100%	C
Item 41	Krug	17,451	$0.17	$2,967	$3,550,479	100%	C
Item 37	Smith	9,655	$0.09	$869	$3,551,348	100%	C
Item 7	Loni	1,970	$0.08	$158	$3,551,506	100%	C
				$3,551,506			

With this data alone, we can construct an ABC table to identify opportunity areas. Successfully interpreting the ABC table is important. Item 24 <u>alone</u> (sourced from the Wilson Company) represents the highest annual projected spending on any one item (10 percent of total), followed by Item 12. Item 24 and Item 12 <u>together</u> represent 19 percent of overall annual spending. Items 24, 12, 8, 56, 60, and 46 <u>together</u> represent 50 percent of annual spending. Per the summary table below, we can see that a very small percentage of items constitute 50 percent of projected annual spending—that's rather enlightening!!

	# Items	% of Annual Spending $	Annual Dollar Category $
A items	6	50%	$1,781,511
B items	11	30%	$1,056,224
C items	47	20%	$713,771
	64	100%	$3,551,506

© J.K. Easterling

So, what is the major takeaway? Out of 64 raw materials, six items represent 50 percent of annual spending on raw materials, whereas 47 parts represent 20 percent of annual spending. This means that a few items represent a disproportionally high amount of dollars. Without performing ABC analysis, the leadership team wouldn't be able to see these results very easily. This example perfectly illustrates the difference between *raw information* and *useful data* for decision making. But how could the categorized data be used efficiently and effectively? There are at least four ideas:

1. Inventory is an asset—an essential part of a company's Balance Sheet. High inventory accuracy is important from both accounting and supply chain perspectives. The six items that represent 50 percent of dollar value could be stored in secure locations to enable higher inventory accuracy. This approach is frequently used in the electronics industry, where some items—such as microprocessors—are a major percentage of a product's overall raw material cost structure.

2. As discussed earlier in the book, supply chain professionals must effectively manage their time as there's no shortage of opportunities. Sourcing professionals could use ABC data for developing negotiating strategies with top-tier (spend) suppliers.

3. Also tying in to a topic from earlier in the book, this data could be used as input to the "make or buy" decision. The executive team could use the ABC analysis to evaluate whether some items might be insourced at a lower total cost than if they were purchased from a supplier.

4. Further reiterating a topic from earlier in the book, this data could be used as input to developing a VMI (vendor managed inventory) program. Items that represent a large percentage of annual spending (or current dollars) is an excellent starting point for VMI analysis.

Senior managers and executives perform various calculations as part of quantitative decision making. Performing a calculation(s) is simply the first step in the overall managerial process. The "3-Cs"[21] approach is often used for any quantitative measure or key performance indicator:

- **Step 1: Perform the required <u>Calculation(s)</u>** - This step involves consistently applying mathematical computations to a set of data. Before performing calculations, steps should be taken to ensure that the data are accurate and reliable. Performing calculations with unreliable data leads to unreliable results that can lead to poor decision making. As noted earlier, this is what supply chain professionals often refer to as *"Garbage In...Garbage Out."*

- **Step 2: <u>Clarify</u> the results** - This step includes interpreting performance versus prior and current internal goals, benchmarking external competitors to gauge overall industry competitiveness, developing improvement plans, assessing risk, seeking input/feedback from other functional areas, etc.

- **Step 3: <u>Communicate</u> an action plan** - This step is especially important, as top organizational leaders must continually implement improvement initiatives to drive the firm toward higher levels of operational and financial performance. Additionally, organizational leaders must ensure that all employees understand their individual roles in contributing toward functional, business unit, and corporate goals.

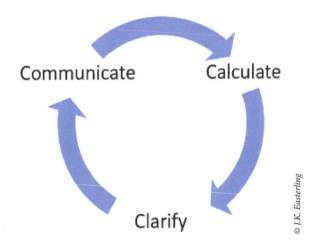

© J.K. Easterling

---

[21] Easterling, J.K., & Barthel, L.R. (2022). Capacity Management: The Intersection of Supply Chain and Accounting. *Business Education Forum, 76(4)*, 11–14.

Project Management

Supply chain professionals must have a deep understanding of project management. A ***project*** is composed of a series of tasks to accomplish a specified mission in a specified time frame. A simple example is the implementation of a new Enterprise Resource Planning (ERP) system (see the *Supply Chain Integration* chapter), which is comprised of multiple tasks (or segments), such as:

- gaining approval from senior management to pursue a new ERP system (this is often referred to as a ***business case***, which explains the justification, or reasoning, for the new system);

- gaining approval for funding (this is referred to as an ***Appropriation Request [AR]***, which establishes an approved budget for the necessary spending);

- evaluation of multiple systems, usually by a team of people identifying pros/cons of each option;

- selection of an ERP system that has the desired features within the context of budget parameters;

- determining the project team members;

- implementation of new system; and

- training of employees.

As you can see from the list above, the project begins with justifying the business case, and ends with the actual implementation of the system and training of employees. At the conclusion phase of the project, the operations phase begins with using the new ERP system day-to-day. In simpler terms, the end of a project is simply the beginning of using the new system in an operations setting.

We can use our earlier example of building a new factory. All the cumulative activities (tasks) that go into building a new factory can be thought of as a project. Once the new factory is complete, operational and tactical activities such as scheduling production, calibrating equipment, evaluating control charts, unloading deliveries from suppliers, cycle counting inventory, and processing customer shipments begins. The illustration below highlights the typical four phases of a project life cycle.

© Yabresse/shutterstock.com

There are many examples of supply chain-specific projects, including building a new warehouse, phasing out a current product (or phasing in a new product), adding a new supplier, increasing capacity in an existing factory, etc. **Gantt charts** are visual representations of timelines associated with various tasks in an overall project. Gantt charts shows the approximate duration (expected start and end times), as well as an overall sequence for each task. Some tasks must be completed before others (**precedence**), while some tasks can be worked on simultaneously. To use our earlier example of building a new factory, walls must be built before the roof can be installed (precedence), whereas the plumbing system could be installed at the same time as the roof (by different contractors, of course). A project is not complete until <u>all tasks</u> are completed.

© NicoElNino/Shutterstock.com

While projects are typically represented by employees working in many different types of roles, the overall leader is called the Project Manager. **Project Managers** decide how to most efficiently (time, people, cost, and other considerations, etc.) accomplish the mission. Project Managers are experienced leaders who have significant experience on prior projects. Project Managers need tremendous leadership skills, including the ability to deal with change and the ability to manage and motivate people with varying backgrounds.

Projects face many different hurdles across their life cycle, including challenges arising from governmental regulations ("*red tape*") to parts shortages to natural disasters. Risks always exist that could lead to **slippage**, which refers to missing the planned completion of a given task that has the potential to be highly detrimental to subsequent (future) tasks. Many projects are completed outdoors and as such are at risk of uncontrollable weather. Project Managers try to plan around periods of time when typical weather patterns commonly exist; for example, in the spring of each year when heavy rains are common. Bridge construction, for example, is often impacted by spring flooding, which is why many bridges are constructed during the summer and fall seasons. However, not all risks can be mitigated (lessened), and as such, slack must be built into the overall schedule. **Slack** refers to buffer time built into an overall project timeline to allow for uncontrollable events while still hitting the overall project timeline and cost projections.

The paragraph above focuses on what happens when challenges arise that threaten the original planned completion of a given project. However, the opposite kind of problem sometimes arises in that a project may need to be completed <u>sooner</u> than originally planned. Think of the earlier reference to constructing a new production facility. One of the major inputs, obviously, to constructing a new production facility includes assumptions around customer demand (see the earlier chapter on *Forecasting*). Major customer demand shifts and changes in the overall industry (e.g., a competitor ramping up a new promotion) are common examples of why projects sometimes need to be completed sooner than originally expected.

Crashing refers to using additional resources to complete a project sooner than the original planned completion. Crashing activities can include working overtime (longer hours), hiring additional employees, expediting equipment and parts (faster modes of transportation), and outsourcing parts of the projects to other companies (contractors). The main consideration in crashing is determining whether the incremental benefit in completing a project sooner than originally intended is worth the incremental cost (**cost-benefit analysis**).

Supply chain professionals need to have a deep understanding of projects as they encounter and engage many different types of projects on a continual basis. Building a new warehouse, adding a new assembly line, phasing in a new supplier, and launching a new product line are just a few of the types of projects common in the supply chain arena. Having a deep understanding of project life cycle planning and terminology is essential for those aspiring to senior supply chain management roles.

Closing Thoughts

I hope you've enjoyed this book and that it's enhanced your understanding of supply chain management. My singular goal in writing this book was to provide a foundation in supply chain that readers can build upon. No book is "all inclusive"—primarily because the pace of change is much faster than books can be printed! Supply chain management continues to grow in importance for companies of all sizes and scopes. New tools, technologies, processes, and systems are continually being developed. Supply chain educational and certification programs are being rolled out at all levels. Integration between supply chain partners—upstream and downstream—are being strengthened and enhanced, including the ability to process payments faster (for enhanced cash flow) while having higher assurance of inventory—even while product is en route.

Supply chain professionals continually take on new roles as the profession evolves in terms of scope and sophistication—from conducting risk assessments and developing mitigation strategies to enhancing overall resiliency. Supply chain directly impacts the "top line" (sales) and "bottom line" (profitability) by ensuring that products and services are available—in the right quantities and right locations—to satisfy customer demand at the lowest overall total cost. Not many functional areas have the operational, tactical, and strategic impact as does supply chain—which we can easily see with so many companies having elevated supply chain's prominence within respective organizations.

Have we reached the pinnacle? We're not even close to seeing the power of integrated end-to-end supply chains. Suppliers are no longer thought of as adversaries, but rather strategic partners with whom information is shared on a real-time basis. With global population increases, just imagine the impact supply chain can have on economies with strategically positioning products and services for people all around the world in highly efficient and cost-effective ways.

"May the wind be always at your back.
May the sun shine warm upon your face;
may the rains fall softly upon your fields and until we meet again,
may God hold you in the palm of His hand."

(traditional Irish blessing)

Thank You

Dr. Easterling's family during his expatriate assignment in Tokyo Japan (personal photo)

Index

CPSIA information can be obtained
at www.ICGtesting.com
Printed in the USA
BVHW020444071222
653604BV00001B/1